Ruby Tandoh's new book brings us over 170 recipes – sweet and savoury – for every day, every budget, every taste, in a cookbook that puts your appetite first.

Organised by ingredient, *Flavour* helps you to follow your cravings, or whatever you have in the fridge, to a recipe. Creative, approachable and inspiring, this is cooking that, while focusing on practicality and affordability, leaves you free to go wherever your appetite takes you. It is a celebration of the joy of cooking and eating.

Ruby encourages us to look at the best ways to cook each ingredient; when it's in season, and which flavours pair well with it. With this thoughtful approach, every ingredient has space to shine; storecupboard staples inspire as much attention as a cut of meat and a sprig of thyme takes centre stage baked into soft teatime cakes. These are recipes that feel good to make, eat and share, and each plate of food is assembled with care and balance.

Including Hot and Sour Lentil Soup, Ghanaian Groundnut Chicken Stew, Glazed Blueberry Fritter Doughnuts, Mystic Pizza and Carrot and Feta Bites with Lime Yoghurt, this is a cookbook that focuses above all on flavour and freedom – to eat what you love.

FLAVOUR

BY THE SAME AUTHOR

Crumb: The Baking Book

FLAVOUR

EAT WHAT YOU LOVE

Ruby Tandoh

Photographs by Charlotte Bland

Chatto & Windus
LONDON

1 3 5 7 9 10 8 6 4 2

Chatto & Windus, an imprint of Vintage,
20 Vauxhall Bridge Road, London SW1V 2SA

Chatto & Windus is part of the Penguin Random House
group of companies whose addresses can be found at
global.penguinrandomhouse.com.

Penguin
Random House
UK

First published by Chatto & Windus in 2016

penguin.co.uk/vintage

A CIP catalogue record for this book is available from the
British Library

ISBN 9780701189327

Printed and bound by Firmengruppe APPL, aprinta druck,
Wemding, Germany

Penguin Random House is committed to a sustainable future
for our business, our readers and our planet. This book is
made from Forest Stewardship Council® certified paper.

Design & Art Direction: Hyperkit
Photography: Charlotte Bland
Food Stylist: Rukmini Iyer
Index: Chris Bell

Thank you to everyone who
helped to make this book happen,
especially Matt, Charlie, Bethany,
Bridget and Leah – for having
such good appetites

CONTENTS

INTRODUCTION

'I'LL HAVE WHAT SHE'S HAVING'
FROM *WHEN HARRY MET SALLY*

Food is good.

Think about the catharsis of kneading dough or mashing a pan of potatoes – of being messy, tactile and free. The daydreams you slip into while peeling carrots, and all the places your mind has drifted to while you've been standing at the stove. The clarity of a recipe can be soothing, being told what to do and when, how to cook and why, and having some of life's ambiguity lifted from you for an hour or two. At other times you might find comfort in the uncertainty of cooking: when the idea of giving up control fills you with dread, the most liberating thing can be to do just that, accepting that sometimes a loaf will rise and sometimes it won't, but trying your luck all the same. Waiting for a pan of water to come to a boil is a kind of therapy – being forced to slow down, chill out and be patient while you watch a shimmer of movement creep across the water, as the heat brings it to life.

And that's before you've even started eating. What is more calming than the first spoonful of ice cream after a frantic day, or the smell of cinnamon in hot milk, or a bite of butter-rich garlic bread? A chunk of Dairy Milk is enough to turn around even the foulest mood. There's the buzz of salty fries eaten on the night bus home, and the curative fry-up the next morning. These things feed my soul. Taking a bite of your heritage, whether that's jollof rice or Irn Bru, will help you grow strong. Eating a meal – even if it's collapsed, scrambled, over-salted or under-done – that was made especially for you by someone who loves you, is the best feeling in the world. When the food you eat is made with care (even if it's just from you, for you), you thrive. And returning the favour, making treats to feed your friends and family, will nourish you in turn. All this is what makes food good for you: giving and healing, taking a break, learning and self-care.

What really makes food soar clear of mere nutrition, though, and detaches it from the language of calories, wellness, sugar and fat, is flavour. Flavour makes food a pleasure. It is taste, then – not presentation or prestige, health or fashion – that shapes the recipes in this book. Each ingredient in every dish contributes flavour and/or texture, nothing is just for show; each flavour combination has been imagined, balanced and tested to excite your palate and encourage you to try something new. I've paired banana and thyme in a soft teatime cake, coffee deepens a sticky rib glaze and cinnamon adds fragrant sweetness to a comforting couscous dinner. Old friends like apple and pork, or tomato and basil, are given a fresh twist in some recipes, while in other dishes less orthodox combinations take the stage – try pineapple curd in a camomile cake, or orange zest to lift a spicy prawn curry.

There are some ingredients – onions, salt and pepper, milk, tomatoes – that we use so much, and so often in a supporting role, that we barely notice the flavour they bring to a dish. Flashier ingredients steal the show, and our kitchen staples go uncredited. In writing this book I forced myself to use these ingredients more thoughtfully and more discerningly, and I began to find even the most mundane storecupboard stock exciting: cans of chickpeas and forgotten jars of spice suddenly became meal inspiration rather than midweek supper resignation. It's my hope that as you work through the recipes here you'll find new life in your familiar old ingredients, and learn a few ways to bring out the best in them in your cooking.

Flavour is ultimately a matter of taste, and there's no right or wrong. If you love my sticky drumstick recipe, I'm delighted; if your loyalties lie with KFC, that's no bad thing. As long as you enjoy the food you eat I'm happy. We need to ignore food snobs and the categories – good and bad taste, slow cooking versus fast food – that are used to shame us for liking the food we like. My job is to give you a few hints and tips to help you to broaden your repertoire, perfect a favourite family meal or see an ingredient in a new light.

A return to flavour is particularly important, I think, considering the obsession with wellness in food culture right now. The problem with 'wellness' is that it's as arbitrary as it is expensive: gluten is public enemy no.1 at the moment, but it could just as easily be olive oil, wine or carrots. The things that save us today could tomorrow be a scourge. The pursuit of good health is fine if that's what you're interested in, but when health becomes all you think about, that's not healthy. I want you to eat without paranoia, or shame, or fear. Eat what you want. Think of the Hungry Caterpillar, who emerged a butterfly precisely because it ate what it wanted to, with gusto.

This book is for everyone who likes to eat, whether you're a new cook or a devoted foodie, a fast food queen or a restaurant critic, old or young. I hope you'll find meals to suit you, whether you're cooking for yourself, a hungry brood or your best friends. It's for people with dream kitchens and for those still using a wine bottle as a rolling pin, for fussy eaters and happy gluttons and everyone in between. In a way, though, I wrote this for myself. Learning to cook helped me to enjoy food again, it connected me with the people I care about and, most importantly, it taught me how to care for, love and nourish myself. Be your own best friend, cook yourself something special and eat what you want today.

USING THIS BOOK

Flavour is arranged by ingredient. I've divided it into five chapters: Vegetables and Herbs, Fruit, Eggs and Dairy, Meat and Fish, and Storecupboard. Each chapter is divided into smaller ingredient sections – for example, root vegetables, or chicken. This way of organising the recipes in this book, I think, reflects the way that so many of us cook. We look for meals that contain the ingredients we're craving; we flick through indexes trying to find a dish that uses up whatever we've got in the fridge; we google recipes that use what's in season, or on sale, or approaching its best-before date. As you peruse the recipes here, I hope that you'll find it easy to pick out recipes in this way so that you truly can cook – and eat – what you want. You'll notice at the end of each section a short list of recipes, and page references, to help you locate other recipes using that ingredient elsewhere in the book.

When it comes to tackling individual recipes, there are a couple of things to bear in mind. Unless there are any special instructions to give, or unusual methods to use, I always write the quantities of each ingredient and how to prepare it – whether peeled, chopped, diced, sliced or ground – in the ingredients list. To save you having to rush to pull everything together when you're in the middle of cooking, it's best to get the ingredients out, measured, and prepped before you jump into the cooking itself. Try to read the method once through before starting, too, to familiarise yourself with it, and make sure there are no surprises.

Good measuring is essential to good cooking. I use a mixture of volume measures (teaspoons, tablespoons and millilitres) and weights in these recipes, depending on what makes sense within the context of the recipe. For baking, precision is especially important, so make sure that you use actual measuring spoons and not just whatever spoon you pull out of the cutlery drawer. A set of electronic scales is a worthwhile investment if you plan to do a lot of cooking: using cup measures for flour and so on is notoriously unreliable, while mechanical scales aren't always as precise as we'd like. Electronic scales will give a clear reading every time, though, and to within a few grams' accuracy. One other tool that I use all the time is an oven thermometer; my oven, like so many, is temperamental, running up to 30°C above or below the reading on the oven dial.

INGREDIENTS

Many of the ingredients in *Flavour* should already be familiar to you, though there are a few less common foods thrown in here too, to give old classics a twist. These should all be items that you can find locally and at not too great an expense. I want my recipes to be feasible and affordable for everyone, filled with the kind of food I ate growing up in a big family. I don't use the kind of delicacies that you can find only in specialist butchers, or delis, or markets – I do most of my shopping in the big-name supermarkets close to my flat in Essex, and the ingredients lists you'll find in this book reflect that. Sometimes you might have to shop around to get a good deal, but as long as you've got a well-stocked supermarket near to you, you shouldn't have to look online for anything.

A few notes to guide you through the way I use ingredients:

- Salt is always table salt, just because this is what most people have to hand. If you prefer to use sea salt flakes, use double the volume.

- If I haven't specified whether milk should be full-fat or semi-skimmed, you can use either. Steer clear of skimmed milk, though, unless that's all you've got in the fridge.

- When it comes to meat, fish and poultry, if you can get free-range and organic then you should. It's not an all-or-nothing situation, though: just use the best-quality you can afford.

- I use large eggs, so the recipes here are usually best made with large eggs unless otherwise specified. You can swap in medium eggs if that's what you've got in the cupboard, but you might want to add a splash of milk or water, depending on the recipe, to make up for the slightly smaller egg size. Get free-range ones if possible, as they'll have a richer taste and brighter, more golden yolk than eggs from caged hens.

- If I don't specify whether butter should be salted or unsalted, you can use either. You might want to tweak the amount of salt you use accordingly.

- Olive oil isn't extra-virgin unless I've specifically called for that. Extra-virgin has a unique peppery taste which, though delicious, can overwhelm milder dishes. Use a milder, lighter olive oil for most of the recipes here.

- Black pepper is coarsely ground unless I say otherwise, and it's always more flavourful if you grind it yourself as and when you need it, rather than buy a pre-ground tub of it.

- Garlic cloves can vary hugely in size, from runty pips to fat cloves as big as acorns. I'll specify when it's important to use a certain size, but otherwise you should just use small or standard cloves, not large ones from giant, premium bulbs of garlic.

MY INDISPENSABLE KITCHEN KIT

Mixing bowls, including a glass or stainless steel one for whisking meringues in

Pans, including one or two large, heavy-based ones for soups, stocks and stews

Large stainless steel or cast-iron pan for deep-frying

Good-quality frying pan and, ideally, a small cast-iron frying pan or griddle

Wooden spoons

Chopping boards

Garlic crush

Peeler

Sturdy masher

Spatula

Heatproof slotted spoon

20x30cm oven dish or roasting tin

Few shallow baking trays

Selection of sharp knifes

Measuring spoons

Measuring jug

Electronic scales

Wire whisk

Oven thermometer

Sugar thermometer

Rolling pin

Couple of 20cm round spring-form or loose-bottomed cake tins

Wire cooling rack

Grater, with coarse and fine settings

Pestle and mortar (or a coffee grinder)

Electric whisk

Hand-held electric blender

Plenty of lidded plastic containers

Rolls of baking parchment, kitchen foil, cling film and kitchen paper

CONVERSIONS

VOLUME

¼ teaspoon	1ml
½ teaspoon	2.5ml
1 teaspoon	5ml
1 tablespoon	15ml

¼ cup	60ml
⅓ cup	80ml
½ cup	125ml
¾ cup	185ml
1 cup	250ml

1 fl oz	28ml
1 pint	568ml

WEIGHT

¼ oz	7g
½ oz	14g
1 oz	28g
1 lb (=16 oz)	454g

100ml water	100g

1 teaspoon instant dried yeast	3g
1 teaspoon table salt	6g

OVEN TEMPERATURES

Conventional oven °C	Fan oven °C	Gas oven gas mark
120	100	½
140	120	1
150	130	2
160	140	3
170	150	3–4
180	160	4
190	170	5
200	180	6
220	200	7
230	210	8
240	220	9

VEGETABLES AND HERBS

AUBERGINE, COURGETTE, PEPPER AND TOMATO

RAINBOW VEGETABLE AND
CHORIZO PEARL BARLEY BOWLS

MOUSSAKA

SOOTHING BAY AND CINNAMON
PEARL COUSCOUS WITH TOMATOES

5 WAYS WITH AUBERGINE

COURGETTE, MINT AND
RICOTTA FRITTERS

ONE-POT RED PEPPERS
WITH CHICKEN

This haphazard assortment – tomatoes, sweet bell peppers, aubergines and courgettes – is what I think of as summer vegetables. It's not necessarily that they're in season only in summer, because you can find more or less any fruit or vegetable anywhere, anytime, if you're willing to buy it imported. Nor is it that they're the only vegetables that are good in the warmer months, because greens, peas and lettuce thrive during sunnier spells, too. It's less a taxonomy of vegetable produce, then, more a rough intuition: these are the bright vegetables, in traffic light colours of red, orange, yellow and green – plus aubergine's glossy deep purple – that make me think of summer, and that even in the winter months will brighten your cooking with a little sweetness, light and colour.

Because all veg is pretty much perennial in the supermarkets, we're lucky enough not to have to rely on the whims of the weather to get good produce all year round. Of course, it's great to buy locally and seasonally when you can, but if that's not an option, just make sure that you pick your vegetables wisely: look out for tomatoes that are heavy, plump and blush a deep red; aubergines should be firm and shiny, and dull skins are a telltale sign that they've been sitting around for a while; courgettes taste better the smaller and fresher they are, with heavy, supersized ones left watery and bland; and yet I find that even the cheapest peppers, mottled green and red as they straddle ripeness, can be salvaged with a long slow cook or a blast in a fiery oven.

RAINBOW VEGETABLE AND CHORIZO PEARL BARLEY BOWLS

Pearl barley isn't as popular as quinoa, but what it lacks in modish charm it more than makes up for in texture and taste: it's a great way to bulk out a dinner with carbs without making recourse to the usual pasta or rice. Cooked correctly, pearl barley grains are plump and tender with just a hint of bite in the middle and a sweet, nutty flavour that sits just as well with earthy flavours (see the mushroom risotto on page 62) as it does with fresh, summery ingredients, as in these rainbow vegetable bowls.

Bring a pan of salted water to the boil, add the pearl barley and simmer for 30–35 minutes, or until the barley is tender. Drain it once it's ready; meanwhile, prepare the veg and chorizo.

To prepare the fennel, first trim off any feathery fronds from the top (you can save these, roughly chop them and use them to garnish the dish afterwards if you want, as you would with a herb). Peel off the tough outer layer then cut in half from top to bottom. Slice each half very thinly across its short width, to give crescent-like slivers of fennel.

Heat the oil in a medium pan over a reasonably low heat and cook the tomatoes, spring onions, pepper, tomato purée and three-quarters of the fennel for 10–15 minutes with a lid on, stirring occasionally. The vegetables are ready when they're tender but not completely cooked to mush.

While the veg cooks, fry the chorizo and diced courgette together for 3–4 minutes in a small frying pan with a little olive oil.

Stir the vegetables through the cooked and drained barley, then mix in the lemon zest and plenty of salt and pepper. Divide between bowls and sprinkle the reserved fennel, chorizo, courgette and radish slices on top.

Serves 2–3

100g pearl barley

1 fennel bulb

1 tablespoon olive oil, plus a little extra

3 tomatoes, diced

2 spring onions, finely sliced

1 yellow or orange pepper, cut into 2cm dice

1 tablespoon tomato purée

100g cooking chorizo, diced

1 small courgette, diced

Zest of 1 lemon

3 radishes, finely sliced

Salt and black pepper, to taste

MOUSSAKA

This Greek dish is traditionally a lightly spiced mincemeat mixture layered with slivers of aubergine, topped with a béchamel sauce and baked until bubbling. In this vegetarian version, I've used peppers and courgettes in place of the meat. Although this isn't a one-pot dinner, it's not too tricky and you can prepare the filling, béchamel and aubergine separately in advance to save yourself a job at dinnertime.

Preheat the oven to 220°C/fan 200°C/gas mark 7.

Lightly grease a large roasting dish and arrange the aubergine slices in it, overlapping them if necessary, drizzling with a couple of tablespoons of olive oil as you go. In a separate oven dish or tin, toss the diced peppers with a tablespoon of olive oil. Bake the peppers in the oven for 10 minutes, then lower the temperature to 180°C/fan 160°C/gas mark 4, add the dish of aubergines and cook everything for a further 25 minutes. Leave the oven on once you've taken the veg out, to bake the finished moussaka.

Heat the remaining couple of tablespoons of olive oil in a large, heavy-based pan and cook the onion over a medium-low heat for 10 minutes, until beginning to soften. Increase the heat a little and add the diced courgette. Stirring regularly, cook for 3–5 minutes to lightly brown the courgette. Add the garlic, oregano and cinnamon and fry for a minute more before pouring in the passata and water. Bring to a simmer, then cook for 13–15 minutes, until the courgette is tender. Stir in the spinach off the heat, mixing until it wilts.

While the filling cooks, prepare the béchamel. Melt the butter in a medium pan until sizzling, then whisk in the flour and cook for 1–2 minutes, stirring continuously, until you have a smooth paste. Very slowly whisk in the milk, then add the bay leaf and cook over a low heat, stirring gently, until the sauce is thick, smooth and piping hot. Remove the bay leaf and season with salt and pepper, then lightly whisk in the eggs.

Mix the roasted peppers into the courgette and tomato mixture and season with salt and pepper. Grease a 20x30cm roasting dish or tin (the one you used to roast the aubergines should be fine) with a little oil, then line the bottom with a third of the cooked

Serves 6–8

2 large aubergines, cut into 5mm rounds

5 tablespoons olive oil

2 red or orange peppers, cut into 2cm dice

1 large onion, finely chopped

2 large courgettes, cut into 2cm dice

2 cloves garlic, crushed

2 teaspoons dried oregano

½ teaspoon ground cinnamon

500g passata

125ml water

150g young spinach

Salt and black pepper, to taste

For the béchamel:

75g salted butter

4 tablespoons plain flour

500ml full-fat or semi-skimmed milk

1 bay leaf

2 large eggs

Salt and black pepper, to taste

aubergine rounds. Spread half of the filling on top, then layer with another third of the aubergine. Add the remaining filling mixture and top with the rest of the aubergine.

Pour the béchamel sauce on top, covering the lot, and bake in the oven for 35–40 minutes, until sizzling hot.

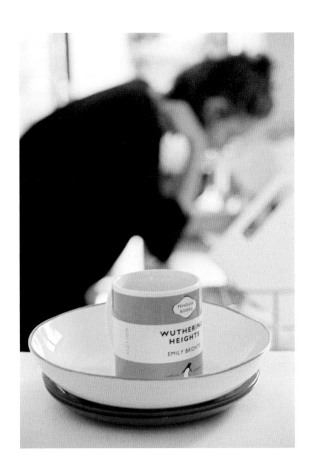

SOOTHING BAY AND CINNAMON PEARL COUSCOUS WITH TOMATOES

Pearl couscous, also known as giant couscous, Israeli couscous or *mograbieh*, is a variety of couscous with fat, chewy grains, roughly the size of peppercorns. You should be able to find it in the World Foods section of your local supermarket or in any Middle Eastern grocer. Here, pearl couscous is partnered with soft onions, tomatoes and cinnamon for a blissfully easy and totally comforting midweek meal.

Cinnamon is more often seen in sweet dishes than in savoury, but its affinity with the acidic sweetness of fruits such as apples, pears and blackberries also makes it well suited for tomato-based sauces like this one. Its gentle warmth tempers the fruitiness of the tomatoes, while the bay leaves lend a deep, savoury aniseed flavour.

Put a pan of salted water on to boil. Meanwhile, heat the oil in a medium pan, then add the tomatoes, garlic, bay leaves, cinnamon sticks, oregano and a generous pinch of salt. Put a lid on the pan and leave the tomatoes to cook over a low heat for 20 minutes.

While they soften, cook the pearl couscous in the boiling water for 7–8 minutes, or until tender, then drain. Tip the cooked couscous into the tomato pan, stir and season well, then serve immediately.

Serves 4

2 tablespoons good-quality olive oil

500g cherry tomatoes, quartered

2 cloves garlic, crushed

3 bay leaves

2 cinnamon sticks

1 teaspoon dried oregano

300g pearl couscous

Pinch of salt

5 WAYS WITH AUBERGINE

It's never easy to predict which way fashion will swing. The ingredients that you can buy only online today might, in a few months' time, be so prolific in the supermarkets, on TV and in recipe books that you can barely stand to look at them. Golden beetroot could be the new black garlic; amaranth could slip out of favour just as easily as gluten could stage a triumphant comeback.

I've found it really tricky to balance that unpredictability – in favour of relevance and contemporariness on the one hand, and timelessness on the other – in this book, and there are plenty of recipes that I've tweaked, overhauled or cut out entirely for fear that they'd be dated by the time that *Flavour* reached shop shelves. It means a lot, then, that fashionable aubergine has managed to survive the cut with not just one, or two, but five whole recipes devoted to it.

Unlike the probably fleeting appeal of acai bowls and kimchi burgers, I reckon there's more substance to aubergine's appeal than simple trendiness. Despite extravagant pricing on the part of the supermarkets, aubergine is still much more affordable than meat, and often just as filling, making a hearty substitute for lamb or beef in soups, stews or curries, and an attractive main course in any vegetarian meal. It's versatile, too: try scorching the skins to withered blackness under the grill; slice it into thin rounds and fry in plenty of olive oil; halve and score the aubergine, then stuff the knife incisions with plump cloves of garlic and roast in the oven; stew it in sweet-sour casseroles or fry with courgette and pepper for a no-frills classic ratatouille.

15-MINUTE HERB-CRUSTED GRILLED AUBERGINE

I have used walnuts to mirror the slight bitterness of the aubergine in this quick, grilled aubergine dish, though you could use pine nuts, toasted almonds or even pecans for a slightly sweeter crunch.

Turn the grill on to a medium-high temperature and have a foil-lined grill pan and rack to hand.

Score a deep criss-cross pattern into the cut sides of the aubergine halves. Place under the grill for 5 minutes, skin side up, while you break the bread into breadcrumbs and mix it with the feta, nuts and herbs. After 5 minutes, turn the aubergine so the cut sides now face up, brush with olive oil and season with salt and pepper. Grill for 5 minutes this way before topping with the breadcrumb mixture and grilling for a final 2–3 minutes.

Serves 2

2 aubergines, halved along their length

1 slice wholemeal bread

50g feta, broken into small chunks

25g walnuts, roughly chopped

Small handful of a mix of parsley, coriander and mint, all coarsely chopped

Olive oil

Salt and black pepper, to taste

AUBERGINE AND OKRA MASALA

Aubergine pads out this vegetarian side dish, so serve it with rice for a hearty main course if you prefer. You might notice a sticky sliminess inside the okra as you cut it – don't panic. It's perfectly normal for okra to be a little sticky inside; this disappears as it's cooked.

Heat two tablespoons of the oil in a large, heavy-based pan. Fry the onion over a low heat for 15 minutes, until softened and translucent. While the onion cooks, fry the aubergine in a frying pan in the remaining tablespoon of oil. Cook the aubergine over a medium-high heat for 5 minutes, turning regularly, until it's lightly browned, then set it aside.

When the onion is ready, add the crushed garlic, spices and tomato purée. Fry for a couple of minutes before adding the water, okra and a couple of good pinches of salt. Bring to a simmer then reduce the heat and cook for 10 minutes, until just over half of the water has evaporated and the okra is tender. Add the fried aubergine and cook for 5 more minutes, to give a reasonably dark, dry curry.

Serves 6 as a side, or 4 as a main course with rice

3 tablespoons vegetable oil

1 large onion, finely chopped

2 small aubergines, cut into 2cm cubes

3 cloves garlic, crushed

2 teaspoons ground coriander

1 teaspoon turmeric

1 teaspoon ground cumin

1 star anise

¼ – ½ teaspoon hot chilli powder, to taste

2 tablespoons tomato purée

375ml water

350g okra, ends trimmed, cut into 2–3cm lengths

Salt, to taste

CINNAMON-SPICED AUBERGINE WITH POMEGRANATE, OREGANO AND YOGHURT

This easy aubergine meal is a game of contrasts: soft, cinnamon-speckled aubergine coins are brightened with tangy yoghurt, sharp pomegranate seeds and hot garlic. Take this to the table as it is in its roasting dish or oven tray, to show off the beautiful visual contrast, too, the muted earthy tones of the aubergine brought to life with a shock of pink, white and green.

Preheat the oven to 180°C/fan 160°C/gas mark 4.

Whisk four tablespoons of the olive oil with the crushed garlic, cinnamon, chilli and a pinch of salt. Pour half of the spiced oil over a large baking sheet, lay the aubergine slices on top then drizzle over the remaining oil mixture. Roast in the oven for 30 minutes.

Meanwhile, whisk the yoghurt with the lemon juice and the remaining tablespoon of olive oil, and season generously. Add a drop of water to slacken the yoghurt dressing if it's very thick.

Once the aubergine is cooked, leave to cool for 5 minutes before drizzling over the yoghurt dressing and sprinkling with the pomegranate seeds and oregano.

Serves 2

5 tablespoons olive oil

1 clove garlic, crushed

1 teaspoon ground cinnamon

¼–½ teaspoon chilli flakes

2 aubergines, sliced into 1cm thick rounds

150g natural yoghurt

Juice of ½ lemon

Seeds from ½ pomegranate

Leaves from 3 sprigs of fresh oregano (thyme will do, too)

Salt and black pepper, to taste

ROAST AUBERGINE CRESCENTS, HONEYED CASHEWS AND LABNEH

Labneh is a kind of Middle Eastern strained yoghurt, somewhere between Greek yoghurt and cream cheese in consistency. Because so much liquid whey has been strained from it, labneh is very thick, rich and creamy but still has a yoghurt tang – perfect for pairing with spiced or salty foods. Usually it'd be left to drain overnight or over the course of a day or two, but a quicker method is to salt it and leave it for an hour or so, then gently strain it through a muslin cloth. You could use good-quality Greek yoghurt if you can't be bothered to make labneh – just be sure to get a full-fat variety.

Mix the yoghurt and salt for the labneh, spoon into a muslin cloth and set in a fine sieve placed over a bowl. Leave to rest at room temperature for 1–2 hours, then very gently – if you squeeze too hard, you'll push the yoghurt itself through the fibre of the cloth – wring out any excess liquid from the yoghurt. You should be able to get a couple of tablespoons out of it, leaving the labneh thick and smooth. Tip the labneh into a serving bowl and drizzle the olive oil on top.

Preheat the oven to 180°C/fan 160°C/gas mark 4. Stir the honey, spices and salt together for the cashews. Toss with the cashews and spread over a greased oven tray. Arrange the aubergine wedges on another oven tray. Rub the cut sides of the garlic clove halves over the aubergine, drizzle over the olive oil then lightly rub it into the flesh. Scatter with the dried mint and plenty of salt and pepper. Place both trays in the oven.

Remove the cashews from the oven after 10–15 minutes (once they're golden brown and sizzling), shake around on the tray so that they don't stick as they set, and leave to cool. Leave the aubergine to bake for a further 15 minutes, until tender.

Serve the aubergine wedges with a big spoonful of labneh and plenty of the honey-roasted cashews.

Serves 4

For the labneh:
250g full-fat Greek yoghurt
Generous pinch of salt
2 tablespoons extra-virgin olive oil

For the honeyed cashews:
1 tablespoon runny honey
½ teaspoon paprika
Generous pinch of cayenne pepper
Pinch of salt
100g cashews

For the aubergine:
4 medium aubergines, cut into quarters along their lengths
1 clove garlic, halved
2 tablespoons olive oil
2 teaspoons dried mint
Salt and black pepper, to taste

CLASSIC RATATOUILLE

There are countless right ways to make a ratatouille – some
are slowly oven-baked, others are spritely and fresh, some are
herb-strewn and colourful while others sink into deep, tomatoey
softness. There's no definitive recipe: this version is just my take
on the traditional Provençal dish, using plenty of garlic and heaps
of vegetables for an easy vegetarian feast.

Heat a couple of tablespoons of the olive oil in a large pan then fry
the onions with the thyme and saffron, if using, over a low heat for
15 minutes, stirring occasionally.

While the onions cook, fry the peppers, aubergines and courgettes
in the remaining oil in a large frying pan. Work in batches so as
not to overcrowd the pan, frying each batch with a little oil over
a medium heat for 5 minutes, until the veg has taken on a little
colour but isn't too well softened.

Once the onion is tender, add the garlic and cook for a minute.
Next, add the tomatoes and cook for 2–3 minutes. Stir in the fried
peppers, courgettes and aubergines then cook over a low heat,
with a lid on the pan, for 15 minutes. Mix in the basil then serve
the stew with plenty of sliced crusty bread.

Serves 4

75ml olive oil

2 red onions, sliced

2 teaspoons dried thyme

Pinch of saffron threads
(optional)

4 red, orange or yellow
peppers, deseeded and
cut into large dice

2 aubergines, in medium
chunks

2 large courgettes,
in medium chunks

3 cloves garlic, crushed

12 ripe tomatoes, diced

Leaves from a small bunch
of basil, torn

COURGETTE, MINT AND RICOTTA FRITTERS

A couple of these summery fritters on the edge of the plate can make even the most basic meal feel special. The saltiness of feta goes a long way towards countering courgette's natural mildness, but still it's worth sourcing the best courgettes you can find if you want the veg to be more than just the cursory 'body' of the fritter.

Coarsely grate the courgette, stir together with the salt and leave to sit for 10 minutes. Once it's rested, spoon the salted courgette mixture into a muslin cloth or clean tea towel, twist shut and squeeze tightly over the sink to strain as much liquid from the courgette as possible. This stage is crucial if you don't want to end up with limply soggy fritters.

In a mixing bowl, beat the strained courgette with the spring onions, ricotta and eggs, then add the flour and baking powder before carefully folding in the cubes of feta and the mint.

Heat the oil in a large, non-stick frying pan over a medium heat. Working in batches, add a heaped tablespoon of batter per fritter, gently smoothing each into a thick circle under the back of the spoon. Cook for 2 minutes on each side, turning the temperature up or down a little as necessary to give a deep golden finish.

For the dip, just stir the yoghurt, ricotta and mint together, season well and serve immediately with the hot fritters.

Makes 12 fritters, serving 4

2–3 medium courgettes (you'll need 600g in total)

1 teaspoon salt

3 spring onions, finely sliced

150g ricotta

3 large eggs

90g plain flour

1½ teaspoons baking powder

150g feta, in 1cm cubes

Small handful of mint leaves, finely chopped

Light olive oil, for frying

For the dip:

150g full-fat Greek yoghurt

100g ricotta

Large handful of fresh mint leaves, finely chopped

Salt and black pepper, to taste

ONE-POT RED PEPPERS WITH CHICKEN

Give peppers a long, slow cook and they melt to perfect softness as they braise in their own juices. Match that rich sweetness with chicken, fragrant garlic and a little chilli heat for a bright and easy one-pot dinner.

Rub salt and pepper into the chicken thighs. Add a drop of oil to a heavy-based pan and fry the chicken over a medium-high heat for 3–4 minutes, giving the flesh a chance to colour. Remove the browned chicken from the pan while you get the vegetables started.

In the same pan, fry the peppers, whole garlic cloves and chilli in the rest of the oil over a medium heat for 10 minutes, stirring often, until the peppers have coloured and begun to release their juices.

Add the chicken thighs to the pepper mixture, pressing it down into the vegetables so that the meat is in contact with the base of the pan. Turn the heat down to low and cook for 30 minutes with the lid on, turning the thighs halfway through. Check that they are cooked through before seasoning generously and serving with rice or soft-cooked polenta.

Serves 4

4 skinless chicken thighs
  on the bone

3 tablespoons olive oil

6–8 bell peppers, red or
  orange, deseeded and
  cut into chunks

3 cloves garlic

2 medium red chillies,
  deseeded and thinly sliced

Salt and black pepper,
  to taste

More recipes with aubergines, courgettes, peppers and tomatoes:
Hearty Tomato, Walnut and Basil Salad, page 100
Lemon Courgette Risotto with Summer Herbs, page 145
Zesty Lime Chicken with Peach Salsa, page 153
Shakshuka, page 190
Ghanaian Groundnut Chicken Stew, page 231
Korean-inspired Rice Bowls, page 240
Sausages with Orecchiette, Fennel and Pepper, page 261
Catalan Fish Stew, page 270
Vegetable-packed Chickpea and Orzo Minestrone, page 284
Hot and Sour Red Lentil Soup, page 289
Kale, Borlotti Bean and Pumpkin Seed Enchiladas, page 293

GREENS, BEANS AND BRASSICAS

CHARRED ASPARAGUS WITH DUKKAH, FETA AND HAZELNUT OIL

CALDO VERDE

'PERFECT PROTEIN' ROASTED BROCCOLI QUINOA

SEED-TOPPED ROASTED CAULIFLOWER DIP

QUICK BROCCOLI SATAY STIR FRY

KALE, SWEET POTATO AND MOZZARELLA PIE

It's no wonder that 'eat your greens' feels like a threat when so often we cook our vegetables to soggy death. Sulphurous sprouts, cabbage boiled to sliminess and watery broccoli are enough to put anyone off green vegetables for life, and there aren't many of us who haven't had to endure one or all of those culinary crimes at some point. It's such a shame, because these greens can be magnificent: broccoli has a nutty crunch, the crimped leaves of savoy cabbage are iron-rich and earthy, cauliflower tastes almost buttery when it's browned in the oven, while even bitter kale and chard can be mellowed by partnering them with cheese, nuts and starchy veg. All it takes is a little care when cooking. Err on the side of undercooking to keep a little texture to your greens and to stop brassicas (that's cabbages, sprouts, broccoli and so on) from releasing that sulphurous taste. Be good to your greens; they're so, so good for you.

CHARRED ASPARAGUS WITH DUKKAH, FETA AND HAZELNUT OIL

Dukkah – a North African spice mix made with hazelnuts, sesame seeds and crushed spices – really complements asparagus, especially when the veg has been well browned to deepen its inherent nuttiness. Little and often is the key to making your own spice blends because they quickly lose their flavour and aroma once ground. You'll need a coffee grinder or food processor to get a good texture.

Make sure you use young, fine asparagus stalks and not the older, woody kind. The acridity of old asparagus has no place in a dish as delicate as this. You can use a good-quality olive oil as an alternative if you can't get hold of hazelnut oil, though you should be able to find it in most big supermarkets.

First, prepare the dukkah. Finely chop the hazelnuts and toast in a dry frying pan over a medium heat, stirring continuously until the nut fragments have tanned a light golden brown. Tip into a bowl to cool. Toast the sesame, coriander and cumin seeds together in the same way until the coriander and cumin are fragrant and the sesame has darkened a shade.

Combine the toasted nuts and seeds with a good couple of pinches of salt in a food processor or, in batches, in a coffee grinder. Pulse in short bursts until the mixture is coarsely ground, with no whole seeds remaining. Don't overdo it, or you'll end up with a spice paste as the nuts and seeds release their oils. Store in an airtight jar or tub and use within a week or two.

When you're ready to make the dish, heat the oil in a large, heavy griddle pan. (A standard frying pan will also work, but you won't get those stark geometric char lines on your asparagus.) Snap off any woody ends of asparagus. Brush the stalks sparingly with hazelnut oil, then set in the pan over a high heat. Leave to cook, turning regularly, for anything between 5 and 10 minutes, depending on the thickness of the stalks.

Turn off the heat, add the dukkah to the pan with a generous pinch of sea salt flakes and toss together with the asparagus. Arrange on a serving plate, crumble over the feta and hazelnuts, give it an extra drizzle of oil and a sprinkle of dukkah. Enjoy straight away.

Serves 4 as a starter or side

For the dukkah: (makes 125ml)

Handful of blanched hazelnuts

3 tablespoons sesame seeds

2 tablespoons coriander seeds

2 tablespoons cumin seeds

Couple of pinches of salt

For the asparagus:

1 tablespoon hazelnut oil, plus a little extra

250g fine asparagus

Pinch of sea salt flakes

1 tablespoon dukkah

75g feta

25g roasted hazelnuts, coarsely chopped

CALDO VERDE

I first learned about this chorizo and cabbage soup while working in a hostel kitchen in Lisbon. We often made *caldo verde* for the guests on days when the ingredient budget was tight but we needed something easy, nourishing and filling. This traditional Portuguese dish is lean in cost and has a satisfyingly trim ingredients list, but there's no compromise on flavour: a rich stock, thickened with potato, and emboldened with hearty cabbage or kale and salty chorizo.

Make sure you cut the cabbage into very thin strips: it's delicate 'noodles', not hearty chunks, that you want in this soup. It's easiest to do this if you stack the leaves, roll them tightly together then cut into thin slices.

Heat the oil in a large pan over a medium-low heat. Fry the onion for 10 minutes before adding the garlic. Leave to fry for a further minute or two, then add the potatoes and stock. Bring to a simmer and cook for 20 minutes, until the potato is very soft.

Take the pan off the heat, purée the mixture using a hand-held blender then return to the heat. Add the chorizo and cook for 5 minutes, then add the shredded cabbage and cook for a final 3–5 minutes. Add a little more water if the soup is too thick, then season to taste and serve with chunks of crusty bread.

Serves 4

2 tablespoons vegetable or olive oil

1 onion, thinly sliced

2 cloves garlic, crushed

4 medium potatoes, peeled and cut into medium chunks

1.5 litres vegetable stock

150g chorizo, finely diced

1 savoy cabbage, very finely shredded

Salt and black pepper, to taste

'PERFECT PROTEIN' ROASTED BROCCOLI QUINOA

This protein-packed dish is what I relish when I need some meat-free sustenance. That's not to say that nutrition is at the core of this dish: what I love most is its heartiness, rich with nutty roasted broccoli and quinoa and earthy cumin, and lightened with the crunch of red cabbage and seeds. Make sure you rinse the quinoa thoroughly before cooking as this minimises any bitterness.

Preheat the oven to 200°C/fan 180°C/gas mark 6.

Combine the rinsed quinoa with the crumbled stock cube and cold water in a large pan and set over a medium heat. Once it reaches the boil, put a lid on the pan, turn the heat down to low and simmer for 15 minutes. Drain immediately then tip back into the pan and leave to rest, with the lid on, for a further 15 minutes. During this time the quinoa will continue to absorb any excess liquid, giving a fluffier, lighter result.

While the quinoa cooks and rests, toss the broccoli, red cabbage, olive oil and cumin seeds together and spread over a baking tray or oven dish. Roast for 10–15 minutes, until the broccoli's softening and sizzling, but still has a little crunch to it.

Set the eggs in a pan of cold water and bring to the boil over a high heat. As soon as the water's bubbling, turn off the heat then put a lid over the pan and leave to sit for around 6 minutes. This time will give eggs that are hard-boiled, but with just a hint of creaminess left in the yolk. Remove the eggs with a slotted spoon and place in cold water for a minute, then peel off the shells. Cut the eggs into quarters.

Fluff the quinoa with a fork, season it then scatter over a large board or serving plate. Arrange the roasted broccoli and cabbage on top with the egg quarters, then scatter over the sunflower seeds. Serve warm.

Serves 4

200g quinoa, rinsed and drained

1 vegetable stock cube, crumbled

400ml cold water

250g young, fine-stemmed broccoli

½ red cabbage, roughly cut into small chunks

2 tablespoons olive oil

1 teaspoon cumin seeds

4 large eggs

25g sunflower seeds

Salt and black pepper, to taste

SEED-TOPPED ROASTED CAULIFLOWER DIP

I toyed with the idea of calling this a roasted cauliflower houmous, inspired by its thick creaminess, garlicky kick and tahini clout, but if there are no chickpeas, it really isn't a houmous. This is a roasted cauliflower dip, then, made by charring and softening the cauliflower in a hot oven to strip it of its sulphurous pungency before blitzing it to a nutty, earthy paste with tahini, lemon, garlic and spice. Do go to the extra effort of topping with the spiced, toasted seeds if you can: it adds a textural contrast and a moreish savouriness that really brings the dip to life.

Preheat the oven to 200°C/fan 180°C/gas mark 6.

Toss 1 tablespoon of the oil with the cauliflower and garlic cloves and arrange over a large baking tray. Roast for 30 minutes, turning halfway. The roasted cauliflower should have browned in patches and developed a rich, nutty scent. Leave to cool.

While the oven is still hot, toss the seeds with the soy sauce, spices and salt, and toast for 5–7 minutes on a clean baking tray.

Pop the roasted garlic cloves out of their skins and place in a food processor with the cauliflower, tahini, lemon juice, paprika and the remaining olive oil. Blitz until you're left with a smooth, thick dip. Season with a good pinch or two of salt, then add a little more lemon juice or tahini if you think it needs it. For a looser consistency, just add a splash of water.

Top with a couple of spoonfuls of the seeds (save the rest for snacking) and enjoy with crispbreads or pittas.

Serves 4, as a snack

3 tablespoons olive oil

1 head of cauliflower, cut into large florets

2 cloves garlic, unpeeled

2 tablespoons tahini

1 tablespoon lemon juice

Pinch of smoked paprika

Pinch of salt

For the spiced seeds:

50g mixed seeds, such as sunflower, pumpkin and sesame

1 teaspoon soy sauce

½ teaspoon smoked paprika

¼ teaspoon ground coriander

Pinch of chilli powder

Pinch of salt

QUICK BROCCOLI SATAY STIR FRY

For a long time I associated stir fries with diets and self-deprivation, but they needn't always be a healthy option. This easy dinner uses creamy coconut milk and plenty of peanut butter for a meal that's as filling as it is flavourful. The nuttiness of broccoli, especially when fried in the sesame oil, sits perfectly with the satay sauce, but you can of course use whatever veg you have in the fridge: beansprouts, pak choi, baby sweetcorn, batons of courgette and water chestnuts all work well.

First, prepare the sauce. Heat the sesame oil in a small pan over a medium-low heat. Peel the garlic cloves and put in a garlic crusher along with the chopped chilli, then press both through into the hot oil to get a spicy, garlicky paste. Add the chopped ginger and fry for 1–2 minutes, then whisk in the coconut milk and warm until bubbling. Simmer for 5 minutes then add the honey, lime juice and soy sauce. Whisk in the crunchy peanut butter and simmer for a further 2–3 minutes.

Bring a large pan of salted water to the boil then add the broccoli and boil for 5–6 minutes, until cooked but still a little firm in the middle. Drain the broccoli and run it under cold water, then shake dry. Heat the sesame oil over a high heat in a large frying pan or wok. Just as the oil is beginning to smoke, add the broccoli and carrot and fry, stirring every 30 seconds or so, for 4–5 minutes.

Turn off the heat, then pour in the satay sauce and add the roasted salted peanuts. Mix everything together and serve straight away with steamed basmati rice.

Serves 4 generously

For the satay sauce:

2 teaspoons sesame oil

2 cloves garlic

1 medium red chilli, deseeded and finely chopped

5cm fresh ginger, peeled and finely chopped

1 x 400ml can coconut milk

1 tablespoon runny honey

Juice of 1 lime

1½ tablespoons light soy sauce

125g crunchy peanut butter

2 small heads of broccoli, cut into small florets

1 tablespoon sesame oil

2 medium carrots, cut into 4–5cm ribbons

50g roasted salted peanuts

KALE, SWEET POTATO AND MOZZARELLA PIE

This pie is a great option if you need to get children (and any other picky eaters in your life) to eat their veg. The excitement of seeing a magnificent golden pie arrive at the table, and then the greedy haste with which everyone tucks into the buttery pastry and dives into the layers of molten mozzarella, means they'll scarcely realise that this hefty pie is packed full of vegetables, nuts and goodness.

I really like the earthy, iron-rich savouriness of kale alongside the bright sweet potato in this pie filling, but you should swap ingredients in or out as you please, depending on what you happen to have in your kitchen at the time. Mashed carrots, celeriac or swede work well in place of the sweet potatoes, while cabbage or spinach (wilted then thoroughly drained) could replace the kale. Other possible additions include feta, flaked almonds, sautéed peppers or courgette, a sprinkling of sesame seeds or even, for a non-vegetarian version, chopped and fried smoky bacon.

Bring a large pan of salted water to the boil and cook the sweet potato until tender (this could take anywhere between 10 and 20 minutes). While the sweet potato cooks, heat half of the oil in a frying pan and fry the red onion and chilli over a medium-low heat for 10–15 minutes, or until it's soft and sweet. Once the sweet potato is nearly done, add the kale to a steamer rack above the sweet potato pan and cook for a further 5 minutes. Mash the sweet potato with the remaining two tablespoons of olive oil, the smoked paprika and a little salt and pepper. Leave to cool.

Roll two-thirds of the pastry out on a lightly floured surface until it's big enough to line the base and sides of the tin. (This is a deep pie, so you will need a cake tin rather than a shallow pie dish.) Drape the pastry into the tin, trim off any excess and transfer to the fridge to chill for 30 minutes. Meanwhile, preheat the oven to 200°C/fan 180°C/gas mark 6.

Now to assemble: spread half of the sweet potato mash over the chilled pastry base, sprinkle on half of the red onion and chilli mixture, half of the pine nuts, half of the mozzarella and

Serves 8

3–4 medium sweet potatoes (you'll need 750g), peeled and cut into large chunks

4 tablespoons olive oil

2 red onions, thinly sliced

1 red chilli, deseeded and thinly sliced

50g kale, thickly shredded

½ teaspoon smoked paprika

500g shortcrust pastry

50g pine nuts

200g grated mozzarella

1 egg, lightly beaten with a pinch of salt

Salt and black pepper, to taste

20cm round spring-form cake tin

50

finally half of the kale. Repeat these layers with the remaining ingredients, pressing everything firmly down into the tin as you do so. Roll the rest of the pastry out to a circle large enough to cover the pie, lay it on top and crimp it with the edges of the pie. Trim off any excess pastry, brush with the beaten egg and pierce a hole in the top for any steam to escape.

Bake in the oven for 30 minutes, then reduce the temperature to 180°C/fan 160°C/gas mark 4 and cook for a further half an hour. Leave to cool for at least 30 minutes before unmoulding and serving.

More recipes with greens, beans and brassicas:
Honey-roasted Squash with Nigella Seeds and Chard, page 77
Mystic Pizza, page 201
Herbed Salmon and Ricotta Quiche, page 203
Roast Chicken with Fennel, Lemon and Cream, page 237
Korean-inspired Rice Bowls, page 240
Saffron Chickpea Pilaf, page 286
Lemony Green Lentil Soup, page 290
Kale, Borlotti Bean and Pumpkin Seed Enchiladas, page 293

MUSHROOMS

HOT MUSHROOM KNISH

CHESTNUT MUSHROOM GALETTES
WITH TARRAGON BUTTER

MUSHROOM AND MOZZARELLA
BRAIDED LOAF

PEARL BARLEY, MUSHROOM
AND TALEGGIO RISOTTO

MUSHROOM STROGANOFF

My sister hates mushrooms, so in the spirit of tug-of-war, teasing, jibing sisterhood, this section is for her. She has a kind of radar for them, sniffing out even the tiniest morsels of mushroom in a pasta sauce or stew. I admire her tenacity, though I don't see eye to eye with her on the subject. I love the deep savouriness of mushrooms. Admittedly, cheap button mushrooms and chestnut mushrooms don't always offer that much in terms of flavour, but there are plenty of other varieties – delicate, ear-like oyster mushrooms; fat porcini; potent dried shitake – that do. By using a mixture of these pricier, more flavourful mushrooms and the cheap, hearty ones, you can get a fine balance of taste, texture and substance without breaking the bank.

HOT MUSHROOM KNISH

This recipe comes from Eastern Europe, via New York, courtesy of Ashkenazi Jews. There's a lot of debate over what makes an 'authentic' knish (should it be round or square? Must it be savoury?), so I can't claim that my version of these little pastries will be the same as those authentic knishes once sold out of vendors' carts on Brooklyn street corners. But, still, I think I've captured the essence of traditional knishes: a soft, rich filling, crisp pastry and homely simplicity. A plump, steaming hot knish really is love on a dish.

You can experiment with fillings as much as you want: add a handful of grated cheese, or even swap the mushrooms for minced beef, fried lightly with onions. Sweet versions filled with cherries, berries and sour cream are delicious, too.

First, prepare the dough: mix the flour, sugar and salt in a large bowl. In a separate bowl or jug, whisk the oil, water and vinegar together, then add this to the dry ingredients. Stir to combine, then knead very briefly under the heel of your hand – just enough to create a smooth, slightly sticky dough. Place in a large bowl, cover with cling film and leave to rest for 1–2 hours. This resting period is important: it's during this time that the flour will become fully hydrated and the dough will 'relax', making it easier to roll out. The vinegar helps with this, too, making the dough less taut and more supple.

While the dough rests, start making the filling. Cut any particularly large potatoes into halves or quarters, then place them in a large pan of cold water. Salt the water generously then place over a high heat. Once the water reaches the boil, reduce the heat slightly and cook the potatoes for 15–20 minutes, or until they're tender enough to prick with a fork. Drain them and set aside to cool slightly.

Over a low heat, cook the onion in a splash of oil with a pinch of salt for 20 minutes. The onion should be very soft and translucent. Add the diced mushrooms and cook for a further 10 minutes or so, leaving the onions and mushrooms softened.

Preheat the oven to 200°C/fan 180°C/gas mark 6 and brush a large baking tray with a little oil.

Makes 12–14

For the dough:

300g plain flour

2 teaspoons sugar

½ teaspoon salt

80ml oil (vegetable, sunflower or olive are all fine)

150ml water

1 teaspoon white wine vinegar

For the filling:

750g floury potatoes, peeled

1 large onion, finely chopped

100–120ml olive oil, plus extra for cooking and brushing the pastry

250g chestnut mushrooms, diced

Salt and black pepper, to taste

Mash the cooked potatoes with the olive oil, to give a smooth but not sloppy mash. Stir in the mushroom and onion mixture then season very generously with salt and pepper.

Generously flour the work surface, then roll out the rested dough until it's very thin. It should be 60–70cm long and around 35cm wide. Keep flouring the surface and the rolling pin as you go to prevent sticking. Now brush all over the surface of the dough lightly with olive oil. Spread the filling in a 4–5cm-thick line along one of the long edges of the dough. Working quickly but gently, roll this log of filling up in the pastry to give a fat 60cm-long roll. Trim the ends, which are likely to be tapered and messy, then cut the roll into 12–14 slices, each around 5cm wide (see photographs overleaf).

For each slice, gently pinch the cut ends to bring the pastry together and seal the filling inside. These pinched ends will be the tops/bottoms of the pastries. Arrange them on the greased baking tray and press each down to a fatter, squat shape – each pastry should be shaped into a thick disc. Brush the pastries lightly with olive oil and bake for 30–35 minutes, until golden and crisp. Serve while they're still hot.

CHESTNUT MUSHROOM GALETTES WITH TARRAGON BUTTER

Mushrooms pair well with aniseedy tarragon in any setting, but I like them best together in the guise of these cute puff pastry galettes, rich with butter and garlic to mellow the power of the herb. You could also make a single, larger, version of this open pastry round, if that's easier for you: just make sure you give the oven plenty of time to preheat and set it to heat from the bottom, if that's an option for your oven, so that the base can firm, crisp and brown before the mushrooms begin to release their juices.

Preheat the oven to 220°C/fan 200°C/gas mark 7 and line a couple of baking trays with baking parchment.

Roll out the puff pastry on a lightly floured work surface until it's roughly 35x35cm. Using a 10–11cm circular pastry cutter, cut out as many circles from the pastry as you can, then stack and reroll the offcuts (with puff pastry, you need to keep those butter-streaked layers intact, or it won't rise). Transfer the pastry circles to the prepared baking trays then arrange the mushroom slices and garlic on top.

Bake for 15 minutes before turning the oven down slightly to 180°C/fan 160°C/gas mark 4 and cooking for a further 15 minutes. While the galettes bake, melt the butter and stir it together with the chopped tarragon. As soon as the pastries are ready, drizzle some of the tarragon butter over each one and return to the oven for 2–3 minutes. Serve warm with a crisp rocket salad.

Makes 12

500g puff pastry

375g chestnut mushrooms, stalks removed, thinly sliced

2 cloves garlic, thinly sliced

100g salted butter

Leaves from a small bunch of tarragon, finely chopped

MUSHROOM AND MOZZARELLA BRAIDED LOAF

There can be a chasm of difference between the effort that goes into preparing a meal and the flavour of the finished dish. Too often that balance falls heavily on the side of effort, but this stuffed loaf tips the other way: it's a beautiful bread, but it's simple to make, in spite of appearances. I've used mild mozzarella here to avoid drowning out the delicate flavour of the oyster mushrooms, but Taleggio or fontina would also work well if you can find them.

Heat the oil in a large frying pan over a medium-low heat then add the onion. Cook gently for 10 minutes, stirring regularly, to soften. Add the garlic and cook for 2 more minutes before stirring in the mushrooms and a good couple of pinches of salt. Fry for 10–15 minutes until the mushrooms are tender then leave to cool to room temperature.

While the filling cooks and cools, prepare the dough. Stir the flour, yeast and salt together in a large bowl then pour in the water. Use your hands to scrunch and squeeze the ingredients together to a shaggy dough, then work in the butter. Knead for 5 minutes, until smoother, more elastic and less sticky. Return the dough to the mixing bowl, cover with cling film and leave to rise at room temperature for around an hour, or until roughly doubled in size.

Once the dough has risen and the filling is completely cool, you can assemble the braid. Stir the chopped parsley through the now cool mushroom mixture and slice the mozzarella into rounds and set aside. Roll out the dough on a floured surface until it's a rectangle roughly 30cm wide and 25cm tall. Arrange the mushroom filling over the middle third of the dough, so that it sits heaped in a broad stripe roughly 10cm wide (and 25cm long, from the top of the rectangle to the bottom). Lay the mozzarella slices on top of the mushrooms. Cut the 'wings' of the dough rectangle into 8 strips of equal width on each side, each strip joined to the central section (with the filling on it) at one end.

Working from the bottom, fold the nearest left strip diagonally over the filling to meet the join of the right-hand strip one row above it. Now fold the bottom right strip diagonally over to meet

Serves 6

For the filling:

2 tablespoons olive oil

1 medium onion, sliced

2 cloves garlic, finely chopped

125g chestnut mushrooms, sliced

125g oyster mushrooms, sliced

2 pinches of salt

Handful of parsley leaves, finely chopped

125g mozzarella

For the dough:

250g strong white flour

1½ teaspoons instant dried yeast

½ teaspoon salt

130ml lukewarm water

30g softened butter

1 egg, lightly beaten with a pinch of salt

the near edge of the left strip one row above it. Repeat, working your way up, until the filling is safely encased in the braid. Pinch the ends of the braid together so that no filling leaks out. Transfer the braid to a large baking tray. Leave the braid to rise, covered loosely with cling film, for 45 minutes or so. Meanwhile preheat the oven to 200°C/fan 180°C/gas mark 6.

Brush the braid with the egg wash and bake for 20 minutes before reducing the temperature to 180°C/fan 160°C/gas mark 4 and cooking for a further 20 minutes. It's ready when it's well risen, golden brown and sizzling. Serve warm, not fresh from the oven, with a lemon-dressed salad and slices of peppery radish.

PEARL BARLEY, MUSHROOM AND TALEGGIO RISOTTO

This isn't a true risotto, really, using as it does pearl barley in place of the usual short grain risotto rice. Pearl barley isn't as deliciously sticky and glutinous as rice, which means the finished risotto won't have quite the same creaminess as you might be used to. It has a beautiful nutty flavour, though, that pairs nicely with the savoury mushrooms, while melting mild Taleggio in at the end helps to bind the grains cheesily together. If you can't get hold of Taleggio, give it a go with some ripe Brie.

Soak the dried porcini mushrooms in the hot vegetable stock for 15–20 minutes.

While the mushrooms soften, heat the oil in a large pan and fry the onion over a low heat for 10 minutes, until softened and translucent. Add the garlic to the pan, let it sizzle for a minute or two then add the mushrooms and thyme. Let the mushrooms cook for 10 minutes.

Drain the porcini mushrooms, keeping the stock to one side. Add the pearl parley to the pan with the onions, mushrooms and garlic, then stir in the softened porcini mushrooms and white wine. Leave to cook until most of the wine has gone, then add the stock (no need to add it gradually as you would with a rice-based risotto). Once the mixture reaches a gentle simmer, part-cover the pan with a lid and leave to cook for 30–40 minutes, stirring often, until the barley is tender and most of the liquid has been absorbed. Add a splash more water if it needs it; cook a while longer with the lid off if the risotto is too wet.

Take the cooked risotto off the heat and immediately beat in the butter, Taleggio and Parmesan. Season to taste. Serve with extra Parmesan and a little chopped parsley.

Serves 4 generously

25g dried porcini mushrooms

1.2 litres hot vegetable stock

3 tablespoons olive oil

1 onion, finely chopped

3 cloves garlic, finely chopped

300g chestnut mushrooms, cut into chunks

2 tablespoons fresh thyme leaves or 1 teaspoon dried thyme

300g pearl barley

250ml dry white wine

50g butter, in chunks

125g Taleggio cheese, in chunks

4 tablespoons grated Parmesan, plus extra to serve

Salt and black pepper, to taste

Small handful of parsley, finely chopped, to serve

MUSHROOM STROGANOFF

The heavy cream in this stroganoff greatly softens the savoury brawn of the mushrooms, for a flavour that's rich, woody and mellow. You can use any mushrooms, depending on what's in season, but you might want to cut 5 minutes off the cooking time if you're leaving out the hardier chestnut type in favour of the more delicate chanterelle, oyster and so on.

Heat the oil in a large pan over a low heat, add the onion and fry very gently for 15 minutes, until very soft. Stir in the garlic and dried herbs and leave to sizzle for another couple of minutes before adding the prepared mushrooms. Cook for 10 minutes over a low heat, stirring every few minutes, then add the boiling water and the cream. Bring to a bubble then leave to simmer for 3–5 minutes, or until the cream sauce has reduced a little.

Season generously with salt and pepper, and serve over pasta or white basmati rice.

Serves 2

2 tablespoons olive oil

1 small onion, thinly sliced

2 cloves garlic, crushed

1 teaspoon dried basil

½ teaspoon dried thyme

250g chestnut mushrooms, thinly sliced

125g oyster mushrooms, roughly chopped

100ml boiling water

100ml double cream

Salt and black pepper, to taste

More recipes with mushrooms:
Red Lentil Cottage Pie with Cheesy Mash Crust, page 80
Roasted Garlic, Mushroom and Goats' Cheese Frittata, page 194
Stuffed Portobello Mushrooms with Almond and Garlic, page 258

ROOT VEGETABLES AND WINTER SQUASH

SMOKY BUTTERNUT SQUASH STEW
WITH CHICKPEA DUMPLINGS

EVERYDAY ROOT VEGETABLE COBBLER

PARSNIP CAKE WITH SPICED
CREAM CHEESE FROSTING

HOT BEETROOT, HAZELNUTS
AND GOATS' CHEESE

CARROT CAKE ROCK BUNS

CARROT AND FETA BITES
WITH LIME YOGHURT

HONEY-ROASTED SQUASH WITH
NIGELLA SEEDS AND CHARD

Root vegetables might be my favourites – they're certainly the ones I cook with more often than any other. They linger in the vegetable drawer, or even spill over onto the kitchen counters when fridge space is tight, yet stay good, fresh and flavourful for days and even weeks. They're cheap, they're abundant, and you can rely on them to lend body and flavour to your everyday soups, stews and roasts all year long. There's nothing particularly exotic or novel about soil-clad root vegetables or tough-skinned squashes and pumpkins, but they're old favourites for a reason, and they're lifesavers if you're cooking on a budget or for a big crowd.

It needn't be a trade-off between style and substance, either; these vegetables scrub up well if you take your time with them. Grubby carrots, knobbly celeriac, bulging beets and crooked parsnips sink into vivid shades of purple, terracotta and gold as they cook. You'll notice the subtleties of their flavour, too, as you start really showcasing them in your cooking: from the earthy smoothness of beetroot to carrot's latent sweetness and the delicacy of tender butternut squash.

SMOKY BUTTERNUT SQUASH STEW WITH CHICKPEA DUMPLINGS

It's totally meat-free, but this hearty stew – laden with vegetables, smoky rich and topped with sticky chickpea dumplings – couldn't feel further from a vegetarian compromise. The earthiness of the cumin-laced dumplings sits perfectly alongside the autumnal flavours in the stew, but if you want a more traditional topping, just lose the mashed chickpeas in the dumpling mix, add a dash more flour and adjust the water accordingly.

Heat the oil in a large pan over a low heat, then add the onion and fry gently for 10 minutes, until they're softened and translucent. Add the garlic, harissa and spices and cook for 2 minutes before throwing in the carrots and butternut squash. Put a lid on the pan, make sure the heat's reasonably low and let the vegetables sweat, stirring occasionally, for 20 minutes.

Once the vegetables have begun to steam, tip in the chopped tomatoes, chickpeas and enough vegetable stock to comfortably cover the veg, bring to a simmer then cook with the lid off for 20 minutes to reduce the sauce a little.

While the stew cooks, prepare the dumpling mix. In a large bowl, mash the chickpeas with a fork until no whole ones are left. Toss through the flour, suet, baking powder, ground cumin, paprika, salt and parsley. Add enough cold water to work the ingredients together to a firm, slightly sticky dough.

Once the stew has had a chance to reduce, season it. Divide the dumpling dough into 10–12 balls and sit them on top of the simmering stew. Put the lid on the pan and cook for 20 minutes, until the dumplings are spongy, the vegetables tender and the sauce rich and smooth.

Serves 6

4 tablespoons olive oil

1 large onion, halved and thinly sliced

4 cloves garlic, thinly sliced

3 tablespoons harissa paste

2 teaspoons smoked paprika

1 teaspoon ground cumin

½ teaspoon ground cinnamon

5 medium carrots, thickly sliced

1 butternut squash, 1–1.2kg, peeled and cut into 2–3cm chunks

2 x 400g cans chopped tomatoes

2 x 400g cans chickpeas, drained

600–750ml vegetable stock

Salt and black pepper, to taste

For the dumplings:

1 x 400g can chickpeas, drained

150g plain flour

75g vegetable suet

2½ teaspoons baking powder

1 teaspoon ground cumin

1 teaspoon smoked paprika

Good pinch of salt

Small handful of parsley leaves, finely chopped

90–100ml cold water

EVERYDAY ROOT VEGETABLE COBBLER

We don't all have farmers' markets on our doorsteps or delicatessens next door: more often than not, it's imagination and improvisation, not expertise or expense, that you need to make a good meal. This simple savoury cobbler tops a rich vegetable soup with fluffy, buttery scones, turning a raggedy bunch of ingredients – a few battered carrots, the rest of the contents of the vegetable drawer, a cheap can of chopped tomatoes – into a luxurious feast.

Heat the oil in a large, heavy-based ovenproof pan or casserole and add the chopped onion, swede, potatoes, celery and carrots. Put a lid on the pan and cook over a low heat, stirring occasionally, for 15 minutes until the vegetables start to sweat.

Add the herbs and chilli powder and mix in the chopped tomatoes, water and Worcestershire sauce. Bring to a simmer then cook for 30 minutes. Meanwhile, preheat the oven to 180°C/fan 160°C/ gas mark 4.

Mix together the flour and baking powder for the cobbler topping in a large bowl, then add the butter and rub it in using your fingertips. Once the butter and flour are well combined, with no visible chunks of butter left, add as much milk as you need to bring the mixture together to form a pliable, but not sticky, dough. Lightly flour a work surface, then roll out the dough to 1cm thickness. Use a 6cm pastry cutter to stamp out eight or so rounds, rerolling the scraps if necessary.

Season the soup mixture with salt and pepper and top up with a little more water if the sauce doesn't cover the veg, then arrange the scones on top. Place in the oven to bake, uncovered, for 30 minutes, or until the veg is tender and the topping well risen and golden.

Serves 4–6

2 tablespoons olive or vegetable oil

1 small onion, finely chopped

350g swede, peeled and cut into 2–3cm chunks

2 medium potatoes, peeled and cut into 2cm chunks

2 celery sticks, thickly sliced

2 carrots, thickly sliced

1 teaspoon mixed dried herbs

¼ teaspoon hot chilli powder

1 x 400g can chopped tomatoes

500ml water

1 tablespoon Worcestershire sauce

Salt and black pepper, to taste

For the cobbler topping:

200g plain flour

3 teaspoons baking powder

80g salted butter, firm but not chilled, cubed

3–4 tablespoons milk

PARSNIP CAKE WITH SPICED CREAM CHEESE FROSTING

'Parsnip cake' might sound like a gross incongruity at first, but think of it along the lines of carrot cake and it should begin to make sense. When grated into the batter and baked with honey, flour and eggs, the parsnip loses that celery-like pungency that makes it so divisive at the dinner table and slides into an altogether mellower sweetness that complements the soft, honeyed crumb of the cake. You can of course substitute the parsnip for carrot for a more conventional take on the classic, though it's worth mentioning that sweet potato also works very well, and adds a little of that terracotta blush that you'd get from carrot.

I like a traditional cream cheese frosting on a cake like this, but if that's not your bag you can try a lighter orange and bourbon frosting instead: slowly add 4–5 tablespoons of bourbon to 250g sifted icing sugar, until the icing is thick and smooth but still pourable, then stir in the zest of ½ an orange. Drizzle over each of the cake halves before sandwiching them together.

Preheat the oven to 180°C/fan 160°C/gas mark 4, and grease and line the tins with baking parchment.

In a large bowl, whisk together the oil, honey, brown sugar, eggs and grated parsnip. In a separate bowl mix the flour, baking powder, bicarbonate of soda and spices. Add these ingredients to the wet ingredients and stir until smooth. Fold in the walnuts and dried fruit, divide between the two prepared cake tins and bake for 30–35 minutes, until well risen and cooked through. Leave to cool for 15–20 minutes in their tins before transferring the cakes to wire racks to cool completely.

Once the cakes are cooked and cooled, make the icing: beat the butter and spices together, then add the icing sugar a little at a time until smooth. Gently stir in the cream cheese. Ice the top of each cake layer and then sandwich one with the other.

Serves 10

200ml vegetable oil

200g runny honey

50g soft dark brown sugar

4 large eggs

200g parsnips, coarsely grated

275g plain flour

3 teaspoons baking powder

½ teaspoon bicarbonate of soda

1 teaspoon ground cinnamon

1 teaspoon ground ginger

½ teaspoon ground nutmeg

100g walnuts, roughly chopped

100g raisins or sultanas

For the icing:

50g butter, well softened

¼ teaspoon ground cinnamon

¼ teaspoon ground ginger

Pinch of ground nutmeg

100g icing sugar

300g full-fat cream cheese

Two 20cm round loose-bottomed or spring-form cake tins

HOT BEETROOT, HAZELNUTS AND GOATS' CHEESE

This isn't a super-quick dish, so if you're in need of a no-fuss midweek supper, by all means buy ready-cooked beetroot (I'd use two packets, so eight ready-cooked beetroots, because in my experience these are more meagrely proportioned than the ones you buy raw). But if your back garden or allotment has yielded a glut of grubby beetroot, or if you want an excuse to warm your winter kitchen with the heat of the oven, it's well worth giving roasted beetroot a go – and far less messy than you might expect. What's more, I find the mellow earthiness of home-cooked beetroot far less overwhelmingly sweet than the shop-bought variety, especially when played up with tart goats' cheese and hazelnuts. It'll make evangelists of even the most beetroot-sceptic of your guests.

Preheat the oven to 180°C/fan 160°C/gas mark 4.

Give the beetroot a quick scrub and chop off any long stalks or roots, taking care not to cut too close to the beetroot itself. Wrap each beetroot in a rough parcel of kitchen foil (use two layers if your foil is particularly flimsy or thin) and arrange on a large baking tray. Roast for 45–60 minutes, until the beetroot flesh is tender and a small knife or fork easily pierces through to its core.

Now, spread the chopped hazelnuts across a baking tray and roast in the same oven for 10 minutes, until golden and fragrant. Let the cooked beetroot cool a little before unwrapping it and, with rubber gloves on, gently peel the skins back with your fingers. Chop into 2cm chunks.

While everything's still hot, spread the beetroot chunks across a serving dish, season generously and toss together with the oil and balsamic vinegar. Crumble over the cheese then sprinkle with the hot roasted hazelnuts and the thyme leaves. Serve straight away as a side dish for lamb or a full-flavoured vegetarian pie or nut roast.

Serves 4 as a hearty side

6 raw beetroots

50g hazelnuts, roughly chopped

1 tablespoon olive oil

1 teaspoon balsamic vinegar

75–100g soft, crumbly goats' cheese

Leaves from 3 sprigs of thyme

Salt and black pepper, to taste

CARROT CAKE ROCK BUNS

Carrot cake was my childhood bake of choice; rock buns were usually the only treats for which we had the ingredients: this recipe is a fusion of the two. It also happens to be vegan, using dates to bind and sweeten the dough. You can drizzle these with a little water icing to spruce them up if you want, but I think the very point of rock buns is their simplicity: squat, lumpy, bumpy and knobbly, and unapologetically so.

Place the pitted dates in a large heatproof bowl and pour over enough boiling water to just cover them. Leave to sit and soften for 10–15 minutes. Meanwhile preheat the oven to 180°C/fan 160°C/gas mark 4 and line a large baking tray with baking parchment.

Drain the dates – now tender and a little soggy – and chop them very finely, until they're almost reduced to a paste. They may even be soft enough to just mash under the back of a fork. In a mixing bowl, stir together the dates with the grated carrot, dried fruit and orange zest. Add the sugar, oil and 2 tablespoons of the milk and stir to combine.

In a separate bowl, mix the flour, baking powder, cinnamon, ginger, coriander and salt. Add the wet mixture to the dry ingredients and lightly stir together. This stage is important: if you mix too much, you risk making the cakes heavy and chewy. Just stir enough to bring all of the ingredients together to make a heavy, sticky but spoonable dough. The resulting mixture ought to be firm enough that it'll hold in craggy mounds on the baking tray, but shouldn't be as stiff as a bread or scone dough. Add an extra tablespoon of milk if necessary.

Spoon out eight mounds of the batter onto the prepared baking tray and bake in the oven for 30 minutes or so, to leave the rock buns springy to the touch, well risen and golden brown.

Makes 8

200g dates, pitted

100g carrot, coarsely grated

50g raisins or sultanas

Zest of 1 orange

50g soft light brown sugar

100ml sunflower, corn or almond oil

2–3 tablespoons milk (soy, if making these fully vegan)

200g plain flour

2 teaspoons baking powder

½ teaspoon ground cinnamon

½ teaspoon ground ginger

½ teaspoon ground coriander

Pinch of salt

CARROT AND FETA BITES WITH LIME YOGHURT

These are something like vegetarian meatballs: little bites of carrot married with the heat of spring onion, spice and plenty of tasty feta. A lime yoghurt dip does a good job of cooling the saltiness of the cheese and brightening the flavour of the carrot bites with a zesty, sour zing. Take care not to rush or skip the salting and draining of the grated carrot, as it's this stage that draws out the moisture so that the little veg bites hold together without sogginess.

Coarsely grate the carrots and mix with the salt in a large bowl (it sounds like a lot of salt, but it's just there to draw the moisture out of the carrots, and most of it will be lost). Let the salted carrot sit for 10 minutes, then squeeze it out – either in your hands or through a muslin cloth or tea towel – removing as much of the liquid as you can.

Stir the spring onions, feta, lime zest, flour, spices and parsley into the drained carrot. Whisk the eggs lightly together then add them to the mix. If the mixture is too dry to just about hold together in balls when you squeeze it in between your palms, add a drop of milk or water; if it's too wet, add another tablespoon of flour.

Heat a little oil in a large non-stick frying pan. Divide the carrot mixture into 16 portions, shaping each little mound into a rough rugby ball shape using your hands. Working in batches, fry over a medium heat for around 4 minutes, giving them a quarter turn every minute, until they're nicely browned and set on all sides.

For the dipping sauce, mix the yoghurt, lime juice and parsley with a good pinch of salt and pepper. Serve with the carrot bites while they're hot.

Makes 16, serving 4

4 large carrots (roughly 600g total)

½ teaspoon salt

6 spring onions, thinly sliced

150g feta, crumbled into small chunks

Zest of 2 limes

4 tablespoons plain flour

1 teaspoon ground cumin

1 teaspoon ground coriander

Small handful of parsley, finely chopped

2 large eggs

Vegetable oil, for frying

For the dipping sauce:

150g natural yoghurt

Juice of 1 lime

Small handful of parsley, finely chopped

Salt and black pepper, to taste

HONEY-ROASTED SQUASH WITH NIGELLA SEEDS AND CHARD

Nigella seeds (also known as black onion seeds or *kalonji*) have a strong flavour and are one of my favourite spices to cook with. You're most likely to have come across these tiny matt-black seeds embedded into the soft dough of a good naan bread, barely detectable until you bite into one and unlock a heady, peppery flavour. Here they're strewn over wedges of roasted butternut squash, a crunchy spice hit in contrast to the soft, honey-glazed vegetable and earthy kale. I serve this as a main course in its own right, but you could add heaps of steamed rice to bulk it out if you're very hungry.

Preheat the oven to 200°C/fan 180°C/gas mark 6.

Peel the butternut squash and slice into four long wedges. Scoop out the seeds, then cut each wedge into short 1cm-thick slices. Toss the slices in the oil, nutmeg and a little salt and arrange over a large baking tray. Bake for 30 minutes in the oven, turning the squash pieces over halfway through cooking. Put a kettle of water on to boil.

After 30 minutes, brush the top of the squash with the honey (loosened by warming it gently in the microwave, if necessary) and scatter over the nigella seeds. Return to the oven for 5 minutes.

Rinse the chard or spinach and place it in a large heatproof bowl or pan. Pour over the boiled water and leave to sit and wilt for a minute before draining. Serve immediately with the sizzling hot squash.

Serves 4

1 large butternut squash
2 tablespoons olive oil
½ teaspoon ground nutmeg
Salt, to taste
2 tablespoons runny honey
1 tablespoon nigella seeds
200g chard or spinach

More recipes with root vegetables and winter squash:
Red Lentil Cottage Pie with Cheesy Mash Crush, page 80
Beetroot and Feta Filo Cigars, page 181
Self-care Chicken Soup, page 228
Carrot and Herb Burgers, page 245
Steamed Beef and Ale Pudding, page 246
Vegetable-packed Chickpea and Orzo Minestrone, page 284
Warm Spiced Chickpea and Carrot Salad, page 287
Lemony Green Lentil Soup, page 290
Family Vegan Chilli, page 292

POTATO AND SWEET POTATO

RED LENTIL COTTAGE PIE WITH
CHEESY MASH CRUST

SMOKED MACKEREL POTATO RÖSTI
WITH SOUR CREAM AND LEMON

BERBERE ROASTED SWEET POTATO

CRISPY LEMON PAPRIKA POTATO WEDGES

CURRIED NEW POTATOES WITH
ROASTED GARLIC YOGHURT

SWEET POTATO, FETA AND
PUMPKIN SEED MUFFINS

TWO-POTATO DAUPHINOISE

When I daydream about my hypothetical Last Supper or desert island dish, I can't fathom it being without potato in some form. Some days I'm sure I could be content forever on bellyfuls of steaming, buttery mash, other days it's paper bags of salty McDonald's fries, or crisp potato rösti, oven potato waffles slathered in ketchup and hot sauce, crisp-soft potato croquettes or fistfuls of fat, vinegary chips, fresh from the fish-shop fryer. I can't live without potato, and these next few recipes are my attempt at pushing it into the limelight a little more, rather than letting it be relegated to the supporting role. I've included sweet potatoes here too (although they're not actually a 'true' potato) because we so often use them interchangeably with normal potatoes, and in their starchy, filling heartiness, they're potato sisters in spirit at least.

RED LENTIL COTTAGE PIE WITH CHEESY MASH CRUST

I love everything about potato-topped pies: the sauce that bubbles up around the edges of the dish and darkens to a deep crimson; the soft underside of the potato topping that absorbs all of the savoury flavour of the filling; the freckled, sizzling cheese crust on top. This one is a vegetarian version of a cottage pie, rich with red wine and savoury mushrooms to boost the flavour of the hearty red lentil filling.

Soak the dried mushrooms in the boiling water for 15–20 minutes. Meanwhile, heat the oil in a large pan and add the onion, celery, carrot, bay leaf and dried thyme. Cook over a low heat, partially covered with a lid, for 15 minutes, stirring regularly.

While the veg sweats, place the potatoes in a large pan of cold, salted water and set over a high heat. Bring to the boil, then simmer for 10–15 minutes, or until tender. Drain and mash with three-quarters of the grated Cheddar and a little milk, until fluffy. Season with salt and pepper.

To the slightly softened vegetables, add the garlic and chilli powder, and cook for a minute before adding the lentils and red wine. Cook, stirring continuously, for 3–5 minutes until the mixture stops smelling boozy. Drain the soaked porcini mushrooms, keeping their soaking liquid. Pour this liquid into the pan along with the chopped tomatoes, then roughly chop the soaked mushrooms and stir them in, too.

Leave to simmer for 15–20 minutes over a low heat, topping up with a splash more water if necessary. Meanwhile, preheat the oven to 180°C/fan 160°C/gas mark 4.

Once the filling has simmered and the lentils are tender, remove the bay leaf and season with salt and pepper. Pour into a 20x20cm oven dish (or any dish or tray of a similar size) and carefully spoon the mashed potato on top. Use a fork to swirl some ridges into the mash (these peaks and troughs will help the potato to develop a golden crust) and bake for 30 minutes. Ten minutes before the end of the cooking time, sprinkle the remaining Cheddar on top. Leave the cooked pie to cool for 10–15 minutes before serving with peas or steamed broccoli.

Serves 4

25g dried porcini mushrooms

500–550ml boiling water

2 tablespoons vegetable or olive oil

1 large onion, finely chopped

1 celery stick, diced

1 carrot, diced

1 bay leaf

1 teaspoon dried thyme

1 clove garlic, crushed

¼ teaspoon hot chilli powder

175g red lentils

100ml red wine

1 x 400g can chopped tomatoes

Salt and black pepper, to taste

For the mash:

5–6 large potatoes (roughly 1kg), peeled and chopped into medium chunks

150g Cheddar, grated

50–100ml milk

Salt and black pepper, to taste

SMOKED MACKEREL POTATO RÖSTI WITH SOUR CREAM AND LEMON

The rule with rösti is that less is more, but I'm happy to break with convention here. Smoked mackerel provides the perfect complement to the potato in these crisp hotcakes, while Parmesan fills in the gaps to give a deeply savoury flavour and golden brown crust. You can have these from chopping board to frying pan to plate in under half an hour, and with a pile of peppery, mustard-dressed rocket, you can make a meal of it for a quick and easy lunch or weeknight supper.

Peel the potatoes if they're large and hardy, otherwise just wash and scrub them. Coarsely grate the potato, gather it in a clean tea towel or muslin cloth and squeeze any excess water from it. Once strained, toss the potato with the mackerel – skin peeled off, and flesh broken with your fingers into small chunks – and Parmesan. Stir in plenty of freshly ground black pepper.

Heat a good glug of oil in a large non-stick frying pan. Working in batches, add heaped tablespoons of the potato mixture to the hot pan and use a spoon or spatula to press firmly into circles roughly 10cm across and no thicker than 1cm or so. Leave to cook on a medium-low heat for 4–6 minutes on each side, until crisp and golden brown.

To serve, stir the sour cream and mustard powder together with a good dose of salt and pepper. Give each person a couple of hot potato cakes, a dollop of the mustard-spiked sour cream and a lemon wedge or two.

Makes 8, serving 4

600g waxy potatoes

3 smoked mackerel fillets

4 tablespoons finely grated Parmesan

Coarsely ground black pepper, to taste

Vegetable oil, for frying

For the dip:

100ml sour cream

½ teaspoon mustard powder

Salt and black pepper, to taste

1 lemon, in wedges

BERBERE ROASTED SWEET POTATO

Berbere is an Ethiopian spice mix with fiery cayenne, a sweetness from aromatic allspice and a citrussy cardamom kick. The quantities given here make far more than you'll need for this sweet potato recipe, but you can put any excess in a small tin or plastic container to use in another dish – perhaps spicy stewed beetroot, oven-cooked chicken or a hot beef casserole. In this recipe, the berbere gives a sharp heat to the sweet potato chunks, roasted until tender and melting into a thick sauce. This is great served with flatbread: tear off ragged pieces and use them to pick up chunks of tender potato.

For the berbere, first grind the coriander seeds to a powder with the cardamom seeds and cloves with a pestle and mortar or in a coffee grinder. Mix this powder with the other spices and the salt, then dry fry it in a frying pan over a medium-low heat, stirring continuously, for a minute or so, until fragrant and darkened a shade. Tip onto a plate to cool.

Preheat the oven to 160°C/fan 140°C/gas mark 3. Heat the oil in a medium ovenproof pan or casserole and cook the onion over a very low heat, partially covered by a lid, for 15 minutes.

When the onion is perfectly tender, add the tomato purée and berbere and fry for 2–3 minutes. Mix in the chopped sweet potatoes, add the water and season with plenty of salt and pepper. Cover the pan with a lid and bake for 40 minutes in the oven. Remove the lid and bake for a further 30–40 minutes, then take the pan out of the oven and give it a quick stir to break up some of the chunks of potato, while leaving other chunks intact.

Sprinkle the spicy sweet potato stew with the chopped spring onion and sesame seeds, and serve with flatbreads.

Serves 4

For the berbere:

2 teaspoons coriander seeds

8 cardamom pods, seeds only

2 cloves

4 teaspoons cayenne pepper

1 teaspoon ground allspice

1 teaspoon ground fenugreek

1 teaspoon ground ginger

1 teaspoon finely ground
   black pepper

1 teaspoon salt

For the roasted sweet potato:

50ml vegetable oil

1 large onion, finely chopped

2 tablespoons tomato purée

3 teaspoons berbere

4 medium sweet potatoes
   (roughly 1–1.2kg), peeled
   and cut into large chunks

300–350ml water

2 spring onions, finely
   chopped

2 tablespoons sesame seeds

Salt and black pepper,
   to taste

CRISPY LEMON PAPRIKA POTATO WEDGES

These spiced, lemony wedges are more slumber party than dinner party in their messy, salty stodginess, and I love them all the more for it. If you can get them in the oven just before you sit down to watch a film, they'll be ready in time to tide you through that mid-movie lull until the pizza arrives at the door. In the spirit of snacking wholeheartedly, serve them with aioli for a rich garlic hit.

Preheat the oven to 220°C/fan 200°C/gas mark 7.

Place the potato wedges in cold, salted water and set over a high heat. Bring to a simmer then parboil for 2–3 minutes. Drain and leave to steam-dry. Toss the rested potato in paprika, cayenne and plenty of salt and pepper.

Peel the waxy rind from the lemon (leaving behind the bitter white pith) and cut the curls of peel into thick strips. Cut the peeled lemon into wedges. Arrange the potato, lemon peel, lemon wedges and garlic in a roasting dish, pour over the olive oil and shake together to coat. Roast for 30 minutes, turning halfway through the cooking time.

Serves 3–4

750g waxy potatoes, peeled and cut into fat wedges

1 tablespoon smoked paprika

¼ teaspoon cayenne pepper

1 lemon

3 cloves garlic, unpeeled

3 tablespoons olive oil

Salt and black pepper, to taste

CURRIED NEW POTATOES WITH ROASTED GARLIC YOGHURT

Roasting garlic replaces that acrid sharpness with a milder, sweeter taste, so you needn't worry about the garlic yoghurt here being too overpowering. It sits perfectly with the heat and earthiness of the dry potato curry. If you can throw in a couple of naan breads and an ice-cold lager, too: all the better.

Preheat the oven to 180°C/fan 160°C/gas mark 4.

Place the unpeeled garlic clove on an oven tray or in a small ovenproof ramekin, drizzle with the oil and roast for 30 minutes.

While the garlic roasts, bring a large pan of salted water to the boil, add the potatoes and simmer for 10–12 minutes, or until nearly cooked but with just a little firmness in the middle. Drain and set aside while you prepare the remaining ingredients.

Heat half of the oil in a large, heavy-based pan and cook the onion for 10–15 minutes, until tender. Add the garlic, spices and plenty of salt and sizzle for a further minute or two before tipping in the potatoes and 200ml water. Cook for 8–10 minutes over a medium heat, or until the water has evaporated and the mixture is almost dry.

While the potatoes cook, prepare the garlic yoghurt: squeeze the soft roasted garlic out of its skin and mix with the yoghurt, chopped coriander and lemon juice.

When most of the water has gone from the potato mixture, add the rest of the oil, turn up the heat and fry for 3 minutes to dry out the potatoes and give them a little colour. Serve straight away with the fresh coriander and garlic yoghurt.

Serves 4

For the garlic yoghurt:

1 fat clove garlic, unpeeled

1 teaspoon vegetable oil

250g natural yoghurt

Small handful of fresh coriander, finely chopped

2 teaspoons lemon juice

For the curried potatoes:

1kg new potatoes, scrubbed and halved or quartered

4 tablespoons vegetable oil

1 large onion, thinly sliced

2 cloves garlic, finely chopped

2 teaspoons cumin seeds

1½ teaspoons mustard seeds

½ teaspoon ground turmeric

¼ teaspoon ground cinnamon

¼ teaspoon finely ground black pepper

¼ teaspoon finely ground white pepper

¼ teaspoon hot chilli powder

Pinch of ground nutmeg

Pinch of ground cloves

Salt, to taste

Handful of fresh coriander, roughly chopped, to serve

SWEET POTATO, FETA AND PUMPKIN SEED MUFFINS

These savoury muffins are saffron-yellow thanks to mashed sweet potato folded though the batter. Feta and chopped chives help to balance the potato's sweetness, while paprika and cayenne add a spicily savoury edge. These are great alongside a cooked breakfast at the weekend, but they're just as good in lunchboxes, for afternoon snacks and for late-night hunger pangs. If you want to enjoy them over a few days, just make and refrigerate the batter and bake the muffins as and when you need them.

Bring a large pan of water to the boil. Salt the boiling water, then add the sweet potato and simmer for 10–15 minutes, or until you can effortlessly pierce the chunks with a fork. Drain the potato, mash until smooth then leave to cool. Meanwhile, preheat the oven to 180°C/fan 160°C/gas mark 4 and line the tin with paper muffin cases.

Whisk together the oil and eggs in a large bowl before stirring in the cooled mashed sweet potato and all the remaining ingredients except the feta. Once the mixture is thick and smooth, gently mix in the feta chunks.

Divide between the paper muffin cases and bake for 30 minutes, or until well risen, springy to the touch and set in the centre (test this by inserting a knife into the deepest part of the muffin – if it comes out with batter stuck to the blade, bake for a little longer). Leave to cool a while before serving either as they are – perhaps with a little salted butter or a drizzle of good olive oil – or dunked into a bowl of hot soup.

Makes 12

Generous pinch of salt

2 small/medium sweet potatoes (300–350g), peeled and cut into chunks

100ml vegetable oil

2 large eggs

150g plain flour

50g ground almonds

3 tablespoons finely chopped chives

1½ teaspoons baking powder

½ teaspoon paprika

½–1 teaspoon cayenne pepper, to taste

¼ teaspoon salt

50g pumpkin seeds

Small handful of fresh parsley, finely chopped

150g feta cheese, cubed

12-hole muffin tin

TWO-POTATO DAUPHINOISE

This take on a classic dauphinoise takes the usual seriousness and stodginess of this rich side dish and changes it into something a little brighter, cheerier and more flavourful. The different colours of the coins of potato – one creamy white, the other blushing a deep orange – adds a welcome contrast, and the sweetness of the sweet potato actually works to bring out the flavour of the thyme and the nutmeg, for a dauphinoise that's more than just one-dimensionally rich and cloying.

Preheat the oven to 180°C/fan 160°C/gas mark 4 and lightly grease the oven dish.

Peel both the sweet and Maris Piper potatoes and cut into thin slices, no thicker than a £1 coin. While you prepare the potatoes, set the double cream, milk, garlic cloves, bay leaves and nutmeg in a small pan and place over a low heat. Once the milk and cream mixture is simmering, season generously, turn off the heat and pluck out the garlic and bay leaves.

Arrange layers of the potatoes in the prepared baking dish, sprinkling over a little thyme and some of the infused milk and cream with each layer. Add a little more seasoning between the layers if you want to. Continue until you've used all of the potato, then pour any remaining milk and cream on top and scatter over the grated cheese. Bake for 1 hour, leaving the potato tender and the cheese golden and bubbling. Leave to rest for 10 minutes before serving.

Serves 4

2 medium sweet potatoes (roughly 400g)

3–4 medium Maris Piper potatoes (roughly 300g)

150ml double cream

100ml full-fat milk

3 cloves garlic

2 bay leaves

¼ teaspoon ground nutmeg

Leaves from 8 sprigs of thyme

50g Gruyère or mature Cheddar, grated

Salt and black pepper, to taste

20cm square oven dish

More recipes with potatoes and sweet potatoes:
Caldo Verde, page 42
Kale, Sweet Potato and Mozzarella Pie, page 49
Hot Mushroom Knish, page 54
Steamed Beef and Ale Pudding, page 246
Gnocchi with Bacon and Dill, page 255
Comforting Sausage and Potato Pie, page 259
Cider-spiked Fish Pie, page 274
All-in-one Basil Cod with Potatoes and Green Lentils, page 295

HERBS

DEEP-FRIED ANCHOVY-STUFFED
SAGE LEAVES

BANANA THYME CAKE WITH
LEMON GLAZE

PINK LEMONADE CRUSH WITH MINT

HEARTY TOMATO, WALNUT
AND BASIL SALAD

BAY BREAD AND BUTTER PUDDING

ROSEMARY GARLIC CIABATTA

HERB-PACKED FISHCAKES WITH
HOT LEMON WEDGES

When I was first grappling with exactly what this book should be, and what it should include, herbs were at the centre of my vision. I spent a long time trying to bake more innovatively, focusing on flavour and trying new ingredient combinations rather than falling back on the same tired clichés. What really made a difference was learning to use herbs in my baking, and in my cooking more generally, in a more thoughtful and considered way. It was a turning point for me. Rather than just throwing chopped parsley at a dish, or garnishing with useless sprigs of this or that, I put the herbs first: a cake pairing banana and thyme, for example, or a salad where basil was the focal point, not just an accent. It's impossible to explore every single use and flavour pairing of fresh herbs here, but what follows are just a few of my favourite recipes that put herbs centre stage.

GOLDEN RULES FOR DEEP-FRYING

Deep-frying can be daunting, but it needn't be any trickier than boiling, pan-frying or baking once you've got to grips with it. It's the process of cooking foods largely or wholly submerged in hot oil and so is less healthy than most cooking techniques, but far tastier and very quick, giving a crispy, golden brown crust and a light, steamed interior. Here are a few tips to keep you safe:

— Never leave the hot oil unattended. Honestly – don't do it. Don't leave the room until the heat is turned off and the oil is safely cooling.

— Keep a close eye on the temperature of the oil as you work, using a sugar thermometer that you can monitor – the temperature for deep-frying is between 170 and 190°C. The advantage of using an old-fashioned sugar thermometer is that you can hook it onto the side of the pan as the oil heats, and it'll give you constant feedback on temperature. Using a meat or electric sugar thermometer (choose one that works up to at least 200°C) is an option, but often they're designed to be dipped in and out when you need a reading, and can't be left in the pan while you're cooking. If you don't have a cooking thermometer, you can place a 1cm cube of bread into the oil: if it browns all over in 60 seconds, the oil is at the right temperature; if the bread browns too quickly or slowly, decrease or increase the heat accordingly. Crucially, if the oil starts to smoke at any point, turn off the heat immediately.

— Keep children and animals out of the kitchen when deep-frying, and make sure that your pan is well balanced on the hob, with no handles protruding from the hob where they could be knocked or jolted.

— Choose an appropriate size and type of pan, and don't over-fill it. Non-stick pans aren't good for deep-frying, as their coating can't always withstand the very high oil temperatures. Instead, use a heavy cast-iron or stainless steel pan, and never fill it more than two-thirds: remember the oil level will rise once you add the food, and using too much increases the chance of spillage, spitting and sputtering, which could cause injuries.

DEEP-FRIED ANCHOVY-STUFFED SAGE LEAVES

These salty, heavily aromatic treats are Italian in origin, and it shows in their simplicity. The two flavours on show here are both heavyweights in their own right, but together – and subdued by the heat of the deep fryer – they marry in perfect balance: the briny meatiness of the anchovy makes it one of the few fish able to stand up to sage's earthy, almost bloody, heft. You won't be able to eat more than three or four of these in one go, so serve as a starter or snack rather than scaling up to a main course.

Heat the oil in a large pan (not a non-stick one) to 180°C, monitoring the temperature using a sugar thermometer hooked onto the side of the pan. If you have a deep fryer you can, of course, use that instead.

While the oil heats, stir the flour, cornflour, baking powder and salt together for the batter. Whisk in the water a little at a time, adding just enough to give a thick, smooth paste before slowly pouring in the rest. The batter ought to be thick enough that it sticks to the sage leaves, but thin enough that it'll just about pour from a spoon.

Once the oil is hot and the batter ready, start assembling and frying: lay an anchovy fillet on the underside of a sage leaf, aligning the fish with the central vein of the leaf. Sandwich with another leaf, laying the sage leaves flat and pressing gently together around the anchovy. Dip the sage-anchovy parcel into the batter, taking care to keep the leaves pressed together.

Using a slotted spoon, carefully lower the anchovy and sage parcels into the oil and fry for a minute on each side before laying on kitchen paper to absorb any excess oil. Cook in batches until all the leaves and anchovies have been used. Enjoy while hot.

Makes 20, serving 5–6

1.5 litres sunflower or vegetable oil

For the batter:
100g plain flour
50g cornflour
1½ teaspoons baking powder
Generous pinch of salt
175ml ice-cold water
20 anchovy fillets
40 large sage leaves

BANANA THYME CAKE WITH LEMON GLAZE

I first paired banana and thyme together in a simple caramelised puff pastry tart, and it's a flavour combination I can't help coming back to. If you smell the two side by side you'll notice there's a common note between thyme's Mediterranean aromatics and the sweetness of the ripe banana. Here I've matched them in a simple banana cake. It's not your usual toffee-tinged banana bread, but something far lighter, more fragrantly delicate, offset by the bite of a light lemon glaze.

Preheat the oven to 180°C/fan 160°C/gas mark 4 and line the tin with baking parchment (this is quite a soft cake and benefits from the protective swaddling).

In a large mixing bowl, cream the butter and sugar until very soft and fluffy. Stir in the bananas, eggs, lemon zest and thyme leaves. It's perfectly normal for it to have curdled a little by this point. Stir the flour, baking powder and salt together in a separate bowl then add this to the wet mixture, folding together until just combined. Spoon it all into the prepared baking tin and bake for 30–35 minutes, until well risen and springy to the touch. If a small knife inserted into the centre of the cake comes out more or less clean, it's ready. Leave to cool completely in its tin.

Once the cake has cooled, unmould and peel away the baking parchment. Whisk enough lemon juice into the icing sugar to give a smooth icing that's loose enough to brush over the surface of the cake. Use a pastry brush to spread the icing over the cake, then scatter with the lemon zest and thyme leaves.

Serves 6–8

110g unsalted butter, softened

125g caster sugar

2 medium, ripe bananas, well mashed

2 large eggs

Zest of ½ lemon

2–3 tablespoons fresh thyme leaves

150g plain flour

2 teaspoons baking powder

¼ teaspoon salt

For the glaze:

15–20ml lemon juice

75g icing sugar

Zest of ½ lemon

Fresh thyme leaves, to decorate

20cm round spring-form cake tin

PINK LEMONADE CRUSH WITH MINT

Infused with the berry sweetness of ripe raspberries and tinged a deep bubblegum pink, this is the midsummer, reclining-on-the-sunlounger, catching-a-rare-ray-of-sun drink of your dreams.

Heat the caster sugar with the 100ml water over a medium heat until it reaches a steady simmer and all of the sugar has dissolved. Leave to cool while you juice the lemons (you'll need 200ml of juice).

With a pestle and mortar or using a fork, mash the raspberries to a pulp and then bruise the mint leaves. Stir the sugar syrup, lemon juice, crushed raspberries and mint together and place in the fridge to chill.

Once cold, strain the mixture through a fine mesh sieve to catch all the raspberry seeds and mint. Add 750ml cold water to the liquid and top up with ice. Sweeten with a little more sugar or sharpen with a dash of extra lemon, to taste.

Serves 6

125g caster sugar

100ml water

5–6 medium lemons

100g raspberries

Small handful of mint leaves

HEARTY TOMATO, WALNUT AND BASIL SALAD

I love the slightly bitter crunch of walnut in this hearty version of a summer tomato salad. Tomatoes are often matched with robust flavours, but here that strength is earthier and nuttier than usual, bringing out tomato's meatier side. Serve this with chicken legs or an oily, full-flavoured fish such as mackerel. For an even bolder take on this side dish, swap the basil for the more pronounced aniseed heft of fresh tarragon leaves.

Toss the tomatoes, onion, basil leaves and walnuts together and spread over a large dish or serving plate.

Whisk the walnut oil and balsamic vinegar together with plenty of salt and black pepper, then drizzle over the top. Leave to rest for 10 minutes for the flavours to meld before serving.

Serves 4 as a side

8 ripe tomatoes, thickly sliced

1 red onion, thinly sliced

Small bunch of basil

75g walnuts, broken into chunks

2 tablespoons walnut oil

2 teaspoons balsamic vinegar

Salt and black pepper, to taste

BAY BREAD AND BUTTER PUDDING

Bread and butter pudding is my favourite soothing dessert. Apart from a whisper of a buttery crust and perhaps the crunch of glistening demerara sugar on top, it's perfectly velvety soft – all custardy, quivering bread and sweet sultanas.

Some are dubious about the power of bay leaves. Because they are so often thrown into rich stews, ragùs and roasts, it's near impossible to pick out the influence of the bay leaf in the finished dish and easy to assume therefore that it's not done much good. That's why it's interesting to use bay leaves in milder settings from time to time. With delicate dairy flavours, bay leaves add a noticeable savoury, almost medicinal note somewhere between menthol, aniseed and tea. Watch out for it next time you make a bay-infused béchamel, or try it in this rich bread and butter pudding.

Heat the milk with the bay leaves, nutmeg and vanilla extract over a low heat until scalding hot, then leave to cool and infuse. While the milk cools, butter the bread and soak the sultanas in a little boiling water.

Strain the milk, leaving behind the bay leaves, then whisk in the double cream, eggs and half of the sugar. Drain the plumped sultanas.

Arrange the buttered bread slices overlapping in a medium oven dish (I used a 15x22cm tin), scattering in the sultanas as you go. Pour over the milk mixture and leave to sit for 15 minutes. Preheat the oven to 180°C/fan 160°C/gas mark 4.

Sprinkle the remaining sugar over the top of the pudding and bake for 40–45 minutes, until golden and puffed. Serve straight away.

Serves 4–6

350ml milk

4 bay leaves

¼ teaspoon ground nutmeg

2 teaspoons vanilla extract

8 slices medium-thickness white bread

30g butter, softened

75g sultanas

100ml double cream

2 large eggs

6 tablespoons demerara sugar

ROSEMARY GARLIC CIABATTA

Every lonely Friday night that I've ever spent at home watching rom-coms, I've been drawn to an emotional fork in the road. Was I to feel jealous of Harry and Sally, Bridget and Mark Darcy, Harold and Maude, for the love they had, and hopeful for the romance they promised? Or should I feel grateful for what I had that they hadn't: the joy of movie nights home alone, eating a whole loaf of fresh ciabatta oozing sizzling rosemary butter, joyous in my own garlicky, unkissable company? I often settled on the latter, in the end, munching garlic bread with happy greed. Let it be the declaration of your love for yourself.

Preheat the grill to a medium heat.

Beat the butter, garlic and rosemary together in a small bowl, then spread a little on one side of each of the ciabatta slices. Grill buttered side up for 3 minutes, or until sizzling and beginning to crisp, then remove from the grill, butter the untoasted sides and grill for a further 3 minutes or so with the freshly buttered side up. Serve straight away.

Serves 4–6

150g salted butter, softened

2 small cloves garlic, crushed

Leaves from 3 sprigs of rosemary, finely chopped

1 x 300–400g ciabatta loaf, cut into 2cm slices

HERB-PACKED FISHCAKES WITH HOT LEMON WEDGES

These summery, herb-filled fishcakes are very soft, so take care to pack the mixture very tightly into patties, and handle them carefully as they fry in the pan.

Finely chop the cod or hake, place in a large bowl and mash briefly with your hands to break up any remaining chunks. Add the egg, breadcrumbs, curry powder, salt, spring onions, chillies and herbs and stir well to combine.

Scoop out handfuls of the fish mixture and press into patties 6–7cm across. Transfer to a cling film-lined plate and place in the fridge for half an hour to an hour to firm up.

Once the fishcakes have chilled, heat the oil in a heavy-based frying pan. Working in batches, add the fishcakes to the hot oil and arrange the lemon wedges in between. Cook over a medium heat for 2–3 minutes on each slide, flipping the lemon when you turn the fishcakes. These can be really fragile and fall apart easily when flipped; take extra care and use a good, flexible spatula.

Serve immediately with the hot lemon wedges and perhaps some peppery salad leaves.

Makes 8 fishcakes, serving 4

450g skinless and boneless cod or hake fillets

1 large egg

5 tablespoons fresh breadcrumbs

1 tablespoon mild curry powder

¼ teaspoon salt

4 spring onions, finely chopped

2 medium red chillies, deseeded and finely chopped

Small handful each of coriander, parsley and tarragon, all finely chopped

1 tablespoon olive or vegetable oil

1 lemon, cut into 8 wedges

More recipes with herbs:
15-minute Herb-crusted Grilled Aubergine, page 29
Courgette, Mint and Ricotta Fritters, page 34
Chestnut Mushroom Galettes with Tarragon Butter, page 59
Apple, Rosemary and Black Pepper Pie, page 112
Lemon Courgette Risotto with Summer Herbs, page 145
Roasted Apricots, Rosemary Frangipane and Marsala Cream, page 155
Blackcurrant Fool Cake, page 165
Fried Goats' Cheese with Thyme and Honey, page 184
Herbed Salmon and Ricotta Quiche, page 203
Garlicky Lemon and Herb Wings, page 227
Carrot and Herb Burgers, page 245
Bright Beef Noodle Salad with Chilli Lime Dressing, page 248
Gnocchi with Bacon and Dill, page 255
All-in-one Basil Cod with Potatoes and Green Lentils, page 295

FRUIT

APPLES, PEARS AND RHUBARB

5 WAYS WITH APPLE PIE

HOT MUSTARD AND BRAMLEY
APPLE SAUSAGE ROLLS

VANILLA RHUBARB AND
CUSTARD POTS

SPELT PEAR CHOCOLATE CRUMBLE

PEAR, BLACKBERRY AND
COCONUT CAKE

SOFT SPICED APPLE CAKE

Apples have incredible staying power: when I was at school my parents would pack them into our lunch boxes and they'd boomerang back untouched each evening without fail; I bought a pack of bright red-flushed Cox apples two weeks ago and they're still sitting serene in the fruit bowl; even the mice that plagued my old kitchen wouldn't touch the apples on the counter. That's not to say that apples aren't good, though. Something draws me to the simple fragranced sweetness of a Pink Lady, and a crisp Braeburn with a little Cheddar is a fine snack. But I've never really been able to enjoy apples just as they are, which is why I've had to be resourceful in finding ways to use them in every cake, pudding, pastry and pudding I can concoct. Because eating apples hold their shape well under heat, they're perfect in baking – particularly in contrast to the crumb of a soft, damp spice cake, or nestled into the pastry of a hot apple pie. Whereas cooking apples, which are tarter and less sweet, cook down to a sharp sauce, which works well in savoury settings.

When a pear is perfectly ripe – just soft enough to dent under the pressure of your thumb, but not so soft that it's slipped into unpalatable graininess – it's a shame to do anything other than eat it plain, the juices trickling down your chin. The problem is finding that elusive pear, though, and too often the ones in the shops are either grenades or overripe to the point of rotting. That's when it can help to have a recipe or two handy. Poaching, roasting and caramelising are all good ways to coax a little goodness from sadder pears, though you could even lightly pickle them (use plenty of sugar and vinegar, and a good dose of pickling spices) or brush with honey and grill them, perhaps with a sprinkling of allspice or cinnamon.

Rhubarb really benefits from a little sweetness and heat to balance its sourness and the toughness of those long fibres that stretch along the length of the stem, particularly in the woodier summer and autumn stalks. What happens when you put rhubarb, sugar and heat together is nothing short of alchemy; the rhubarb sliding into sweet-sharp, delicate tenderness, almost in spite of itself. Even the toughest old plants will yield, with a little sweetness.

5 WAYS WITH APPLE PIE

Apple pie is hard to get wrong, but it's hard to master, too. There's no right way to make it but the crust should be buttery and short, the underneath rich with juice; the apples should be a mixture of tart cooking apples and firmer eating apples, for a perfect balance of acidity and sweetness. Here are a few attempts at that perfect apple pie: none a definitive recipe, by any means, but my best shot at a classic.

SHORTCRUST APPLE PIE

This no-frills apple pie is the root recipe for each of the variations that follow. Obviously it's my job to give a few pointers towards how to make a good shortcrust pastry but, honestly, if your hunger won't wait, just use a packet of all-butter shop-bought pastry. It won't be as tender or buttery as one you make at home, but by the time it's custard-sodden and piled onto a fork with plenty of sticky apple, you might not notice the difference.

Stir the flour and salt together in a large bowl, then rub in the butter using your fingertips until there are no chunks left. Add the water and 'cut' it into the butter and flour mixture, stopping when the pastry starts to come together in clumps and no dry flour remains. Gather the pastry into a ball, press into a flattish round and wrap in cling film. Refrigerate for 30 minutes or so, giving the dough a chance to rest and grow less sticky.

Cut off a third of the chilled pastry and return it to the fridge, again wrapped in cling film. On a lightly floured surface, roll the remaining two-thirds out to a circle large enough to line the pie dish. Drape the pastry over the rolling pin, to lift it without tearing, then gently lower it into the pie dish and press firmly into the bottom and sides. Chill in the fridge for 30 minutes, preheating the oven to 200°C/fan 180°C/gas mark 6 in the meantime.

While the oven preheats and the pastry case rests, prepare the filling. Peel, core and thickly slice the apples. In a large bowl, stir the sugar, cornflour and cinnamon together then toss through the apple segments, coating the fruit completely.

Serves 8–10

350g plain flour

Generous pinch of salt

175g salted butter, firm but not fridge-cold, cubed

40–50ml cold water

3 Cox or Braeburn apples

3 Granny Smith or Bramley apples

65g soft light brown sugar

2 tablespoons cornflour

½ teaspoon ground cinnamon

1 large egg

1 tablespoon milk

Large pie dish, 26–29cm in diameter at its rim

Spread the apple filling over the pastry base then roll out the smaller piece of pastry to a circle large enough to form a lid for the pie. Lay the lid over the apples and pinch it together with the pastry sides. Trim any excess pastry and crimp the edge of the pie if you feel like it. Beat the egg and milk together to glaze, and brush sparingly over the top of the pie. Pierce a few holes in the lid to let any steam escape during cooking.

Bake for 25 minutes then reduce the temperature to 180°C/fan 160°C/gas mark 4 and cook for a further 30–35 minutes, until golden brown and bubbling. Leave to cool for at least 20 minutes before eating with custard.

BLACKBERRY AND MARZIPAN APPLE PIE

Follow the recipe on the previous page, but toss 225g halved blackberries into the apple mixture. Roll 250g marzipan into a circle just large enough to fit the top of the pie dish and use to cover the apples and blackberries. Top with the pastry lid and bake as instructed.

APPLE, ROSEMARY AND BLACK PEPPER APPLE PIE

Heady rosemary works well with the sweet fruit filling of an apple pie, especially with the help of a little black pepper to impart heat. You can also use thyme if you prefer, but I find that rosemary's better at weathering the heat of the oven. To make this version, add the roughly chopped leaves from 3 sprigs of rosemary to the apple mixture, along with a grinding of black pepper.

WHOLEMEAL OAT CRUST APPLE PIE

Reduce the amount of flour in the pastry to 300g, using 150g plain flour and 150g wholemeal flour. Stir in 100g rolled oats (the cheaper and finer, the better – anything too coarse will make the pastry brittle and difficult to roll) after you've rubbed in the butter. Chill, roll, fill and bake as on the previous page.

CHEDDAR CRUST APPLE PIE

Apples and cheese are no strangers, but here's a sweeter match than you'd find in the usual Ploughman's lunch. Make everything exactly as instructed on page 111, but add 150g grated mature Cheddar to the pastry mixture after you've combined the flour and butter. It's best to leave the added salt out of the pastry, too. You can even sprinkle a little extra Cheddar over the apple filling before you put the pastry on top for an extra kick.

HOT MUSTARD AND BRAMLEY APPLE SAUSAGE ROLLS

Lots of sausage roll recipes call for pricey butchers' sausages, but it's just as easy to make the sausage filling yourself, and it gives you far more control over exactly what goes into the sausage meat. I've flavoured these ones with grainy mustard and the fruity sweetness of green apples – natural partners for pork – but you could mix things up with smoked paprika, cooked red onion or even a mixture of pork and beef for a meatier snack.

Preheat the oven to 200°C/fan 180°C/gas mark 6 and line a large baking tray with baking parchment.

Mix the pork mince with the breadcrumbs, mustard, thyme, allspice, salt and pepper in a large bowl, squeezing everything together in your palms to break up the mince. Peel and core the apple, then dice into cubes no larger than 5mm across. Add the diced apple to the sausage mixture and stir to combine.

Roll out the pastry on a well-floured work surface to a rectangle roughly 50x25cm. Cut into four smaller rectangles along its length, giving a set of 12.5x25cm rectangles. Divide the sausage filling into four. Using your hands, form a quarter of the filling mixture into a sausage shape and place off-centre along the length of one of the dough rectangles. Fold the pastry over the sausage to give a 25cm long roll, then press the pastry together, seal with a fork and trim it. If the dough isn't sticking to itself, wet it with a little water or some of the egg wash. Cut the roll into six smaller pieces. Repeat with the remaining sausage mixture and pastry.

Arrange the mini sausage rolls on the prepared baking tray and brush liberally with egg wash. Bake for 30 minutes, until the pastry is flaky and golden, and the meat is cooked through.

Makes 24 mini sausage rolls

500g fatty pork mince

50g white breadcrumbs

1½ tablespoons wholegrain mustard

2 teaspoons dried thyme

1 teaspoon ground allspice

¾ teaspoon salt

½ teaspoon ground white pepper

1 medium Bramley apple

500g all-butter puff pastry

1 egg, beaten with a pinch of salt

VANILLA RHUBARB AND CUSTARD POTS

Woody summer rhubarb is good for crumbles and pies, where its green sourness can mellow and its fibrous texture soften over the course of a long, slow bake, but it's young forced rhubarb that you'll want here – the very fine, pink-flushed type that shoots upwards in tender stalks, nursed in darkened greenhouses through February and March. It's sweeter and more delicate than the summer varieties, and its deep-pink colour is as striking as its sweet-sharp bite. Rhubarb and custard isn't the most imaginative pairing, but this is the best way to showcase the stems when they're this good.

Preheat the oven to 180°C/fan 160°C/gas mark 4. Rinse the rhubarb chunks just to moisten them, then shake off any excess water. Stir the sugar and vanilla seeds together then toss the rhubarb chunks in the mixture. Arrange the rhubarb in a baking dish, sprinkling any leftover sugar on the top. Bake for 15–20 minutes until the fruit is completely tender.

While the rhubarb is cooking, heat the milk with the vanilla seeds (it doesn't hurt to throw the emptied pod in, too) in a small pan until it's scalding hot (but not boiling). Mix the egg yolks, caster sugar and cornflour together in a large mixing bowl, then pour in the milk in a thin stream, whisking as you go. (Always add the milk to the egg yolks, and not the other way round, or the custard will curdle.) Decant the custard back into the pan and set over a very low heat, stirring continuously, until it's thickened to a creamy but pourable consistency. Pluck out the vanilla pod and leave the custard to cool to room temperature.

Fill your ramekins first with the rhubarb, then top with the cooled custard, drizzling over any sweet-sharp pink juices from the baking dish at the end. Place in the fridge to chill, then eat once they're cold and slightly thickened.

Serves 4

400g rhubarb, cut into
  5cm chunks
75g caster sugar
Seeds from ½ vanilla pod,
  split along its length

For the custard:
350ml full-fat milk
Seeds from ½ vanilla pod,
  split along its length
4 egg yolks
100g caster sugar
2 tablespoons cornflour

4 individual ramekins

SPELT PEAR CHOCOLATE CRUMBLE

Chocolate chunks are strewn through the buttery topping of this pear crumble. You can swap in plain flour in place of the wholemeal spelt flour if you want, but I think the spelt imparts a welcome nuttiness that sits well with the fruit.

Preheat the oven to 180°C/fan 160°C/gas mark 4.

Toss the pears together with the sugar, flour and cinnamon and pour into the baking dish or tin. In a mixing bowl, rub the butter into the flour until no chunks of butter are left. Stir in the sugar and chocolate chunks, then sprinkle this crumble mixture over the filling in a thick layer.

Bake for 40–45 minutes, or until the pears are tender, the juices bubbling through and the crumble golden brown. Enjoy hot, with a good vanilla ice cream.

Serves 6–8

8 medium dessert pears (such as Rocha or Comice), peeled, cored and cut into chunks

75g soft light brown sugar

3 tablespoons wholemeal spelt flour

½ teaspoon ground cinnamon

For the crumble topping:

110g salted butter, cubed, at room temperature

225g wholemeal spelt flour

110g soft light brown sugar

100g dark chocolate, cut into small chunks

Deep 25-30cm round oven dish

PEAR, BLACKBERRY AND COCONUT CAKE

Conference pears work well in this cake, though any variety is fine as long they are perfectly ripe and tender. You can find nibbed (or pearl) sugar online, but crunchy demerara sugar is a good substitute. The flavour of coconut oil is the perfect complement to the desiccated coconut here, but margarine is a fine alternative if that's all you can get hold of.

Preheat the oven to 180°C/fan 160°C/gas mark 4. Grease the cake tin and line the base with baking parchment.

Beat the coconut oil, sugar, desiccated coconut and vanilla extract together until smooth and creamy. Add the eggs one at a time, mixing well as you go. In a separate bowl, stir the flour, baking powder and salt together then add to the wet ingredients and fold in to get a thick batter.

Peel and core the pears, then cut into 1–1½cm chunks. Halve the blackberries. Fold three-quarters of the fruit very gently through the batter, taking care not to crush the blackberries as you go. Spoon into the prepared cake tin and smooth the surface. Scatter the remaining fruit on top and sprinkle over the nibbed or demerara sugar.

Bake for 50 minutes, or until a small knife inserted into the centre of the cake comes out clean. I like to serve this while it's still slightly warm, cut into generous wedges, with ice cream. It's just as good cold, though.

Serves 8–10

100g coconut oil, soft but not melted

100g soft light brown sugar

50g desiccated coconut

1 teaspoon vanilla extract

2 large eggs

175g plain flour

2½ teaspoons baking powder

Pinch of salt

2–3 ripe pears (about 350g total)

175g blackberries

1–2 tablespoons nibbed or demerara sugar

20cm round spring-form cake tin

SOFT SPICED APPLE CAKE

This is the kind of cake that's meant to be thrown together – a patchwork of substitutions and amendments, pulled together with whatever you happen to have in the cupboard at the time. The ingredients list looks long but it's mainly the spices that take up all that page space, and if you want to keep things simple you can swap in 3 teaspoons of mixed spice, which is more or less the same thing anyway, albeit less fragrant and of course not with quite the same depth of flavour as a homemade spice blend.

Preheat the oven to 180°C/fan 160°C/gas mark 4, and grease and line the base of the cake tin with baking parchment.

Beat together the butter and sugar until light and fluffy, then add the eggs one at a time, beating well after each addition. Add all of the dry ingredients, from the plain flour through to the salt. Stir until the batter is smooth, then fold in three-quarters of the diced apple.

Spoon the batter into the prepared tin, scatter the remaining apple chunks over the top and lightly pat them in, then sprinkle with the demerara sugar. Bake for 35–45 minutes, or until a small knife inserted into the centre of the cake comes out clean. Leave to cool completely before serving.

Serves 8

150g unsalted butter, softened

150g soft light brown sugar

2 large eggs

75g plain flour

75g wholemeal flour

1½ teaspoons baking powder

1 teaspoon ground cinnamon

1 teaspoon ground ginger

3 cardamom pods, seeds only, crushed

½ teaspoon ground coriander

¼ teaspoon ground white pepper

¼ teaspoon ground allspice

¼ teaspoon ground nutmeg

Pinch of salt

2 medium Braeburn or Cox apples, peeled, cored and cut into dice no larger than 1cm

1–2 tablespoons demerara sugar, to sprinkle

20cm round springform or loose-bottomed cake tin

More recipes with apple, pear and rhubarb:
Harry Styles's Dutch Baby with Cinnamon Rhubarb, page 198

TROPICAL FRUIT

CRISP FRIED SEA BASS WITH
COCONUT RICE AND MANGO

PINEAPPLE CURD

SUMMER PINEAPPLE
CAMOMILE CAKE

ROASTED BANANAS

CINNAMON BANANA TEA LOAF

BANANA SESAME FRITTERS
WITH BALSAMIC CARAMEL

WHITE CHOCOLATE AND
PASSION FRUIT POTS

There are plenty of tropical fruit-based recipes from the sun- and rain-drenched places where these crops actually lay down their roots, but I'm aware that here under greyer skies we're guilty of doing wrong by the cuisines from which we take our inspiration, plucking these recipes and rebranding them as our own. I'll take a more tangential approach, then, fitting these fruits – from bananas to mangoes and spiky pineapple – into the recipes, dishes and ways of cooking that we're familiar with.

I'd love to be able to give a few tips about where and when to find really great tropical fruit, but the truth is that you'll be hard pressed to find anything mind-blowing without taking a long-haul flight. Fruit here – even the more pedestrian cherries, apples and plums – just doesn't have the intensity of flavour that you can find in warmer climes. That's not to say that you can't make the most of what we have, though, and good flavour really isn't out of reach; you just have to be a bit more resourceful with cooking, seasoning and sweetening.

Steer clear of rock-hard pineapples if that's all you can find in the shops (they're closer to weaponry than sustenance), or if you do buy them give them plenty of time to ripen at home. Otherwise tinned pineapple, though often oversweet, is a fine alternative to the under-ripe fresh stuff. As for mangoes, pick the sunnily yellow-orange Indian alphonso mangoes when they're in season in May and June; take care not to go for temptingly soft fruit which, though sweeter and more fragrant, are a pain to peel and cut. Passion fruit works counter-intuitively: at their best when the skin is withered and dimpled all over, these wizened, riper fruits carrying the brightest, sweetest pulp.

CRISP FRIED SEA BASS WITH COCONUT RICE AND MANGO

Sea bass is a firm, sweet fish, so makes a good match for the brightness of mango, coriander and lime. Fry the fish on a good high heat, leaving the skin on for a crisp, well-browned outside to contrast with the tender flesh and sticky coconut rice. A tip: if you soak the spring onions in ice-cold water after you've cut them, they'll twist into pretty curls.

First, prepare the coconut rice. Wash the rice thoroughly under cold water, until the water runs clear. In a medium, heavy-based pan combine the rice with the coconut milk and a good pinch of salt. Bring to a simmer then cover with a tight-fitting lid, turn the heat as low as it'll go and leave to cook, untouched, for 15–20 minutes, or until the rice is tender and the liquid has been absorbed.

While the rice cooks, prepare the mango, spring onions, chillies, lime and coriander as detailed. Arrange these colourful accompaniments in four shallow bowls, leaving room for the rice and fish.

Once the bowls are ready and the rice is nearly done, fry the fish: pat the fillets dry with kitchen paper and heat a little oil in a large, non-stick frying pan. Fry the sea bass over a medium-high heat for 2 minutes on each side, giving a crisp, golden brown skin and flesh that flakes under your fork. Add one piece of fish to each bowl along with a portion of the coconut rice, and serve straight away.

Serves 4

200g basmati and wild rice

1 x 400ml can coconut milk

Pinch of salt

1 large mango, peeled and sliced into long crescents

4 spring onions, trimmed and finely sliced lengthways

2 medium-sized red chillies, deseeded and sliced into fine matchsticks

1 lime, cut into eight wedges

Small bunch of coriander leaves

4 sea bass fillets, skin on

Oil, for frying

SUMMER PINEAPPLE CAMOMILE CAKE

This mellow camomile cake sits perfectly with the sharpness of a thick layer of bright pineapple curd (see following recipe). You can use camomile teabags if you can't find the loose stuff – just swap in one per tablespoon of the dried camomile buds. It's less potent, though, so give the tea plenty of time to steep and do source loose camomile if you can. Health food shops sometimes have it, or look online.

Preheat the oven to 180°C/fan 160°C/gas mark 4. Grease and line the cake tins with baking parchment.

Combine the butter, milk and dried camomile in a pan and set over a low heat until the butter has completely melted and the mixture has just begun to simmer. Remove from the heat and leave to cool and infuse for 5 minutes or so before straining into a large mixing bowl, leaving the camomile flowers behind while squeezing as much liquid from them as possible.

Add the sugar, lemon zest and vanilla extract to the infused butter mixture and whisk to combine. Add the eggs one at a time, mixing well between each addition. In a separate bowl, mix the flour, baking powder and salt before adding this dry mixture to the wet ingredients. Whisk until the batter is smooth then divide it between the two prepared tins. Bake the cakes for 25–30 minutes, or until well-risen and golden brown. A small knife inserted into the middle of each cake should emerge clean. Leave the cakes to cool in their tins before unmoulding.

To prepare the icing, melt the butter with the camomile in a small pan over a low heat until the butter starts to bubble. Remove from the heat and leave to cool for 10 minutes before straining the butter through a sieve to remove the camomile. While the butter cools a little, chop the white chocolate into small chunks and melt in a heatproof bowl set over a pan of simmering water (making sure the bottom of the bowl doesn't touch the water). Stir the melted white chocolate into the slightly cooled, strained butter and leave to cool again to room temperature.

Once the butter and chocolate mixture is cooled, place the icing in the fridge for 20 minutes to firm to the consistency of softened, creamed butter. Stir it at 5-minute intervals to avoid

Serves 10–12

250g unsalted butter

100ml milk

6 tablespoons dried camomile flowers

300g caster sugar

Zest of ½ lemon

2 teaspoons vanilla extract

4 large eggs

350g plain flour

3 teaspoons baking powder

¼ teaspoon salt

For the icing:

75g unsalted butter

2 tablespoons dried camomile flowers

100g white chocolate

65g icing sugar

Zest of ½ lemon

15–25ml milk, if needed

3–4 tablespoons Pineapple Curd (see page 129)

Two 20cm round loose-bottomed or spring-form cake tins

lumpiness. Once it's thick and smooth, sift in the icing sugar and lemon zest and gently stir together to combine. Add a dash of milk if necessary to give a spreadable buttercream thickness.

Smooth the pineapple curd over one of the cake layers, sandwich with the other cake and then ice the top generously with the camomile buttercream. Decorate the top, if you feel like it, with a bit more pineapple curd or even a sprinkling of dried camomile flowers.

PINEAPPLE CURD

I like to use this curd as a filling for the camomile cake preceding this recipe, but it's just as good on toast, swirled through ice cream, or folded into softly whipped cream. Store any excess in a sterilised jar for up to 1 week in the fridge.

This is a pretty standard curd recipe, so feel free to use it as a template for lemon, lime, grapefruit or even blackcurrant curds. Just adjust the amount of sugar to taste.

Whisk the egg yolks, cornflour and sugar together in a small pan then slowly add the pineapple and lemon juices.

Set the pan over a low heat and stir continuously for 5–10 minutes, or as long as it takes for the curd to reach the consistency of very thick custard. It'll be resolutely liquid for the first few minutes, but don't give up on it. As soon as it's ready and about to start bubbling, remove it from the heat, stir in the butter until melted, then leave to cool to room temperature.

Makes 125ml

2 large egg yolks

1½ tablespoons cornflour

40g caster sugar

100ml fresh pineapple juice

Juice of 1 lemon

1 tablespoon unsalted butter

ROASTED BANANAS

The natural sweetness of ripe bananas mellows into a fudgy, fragrant stickiness when you roast them in their skins. You could also barbecue them in foil, for an easy summer pudding.

Preheat the oven to 180°C/fan 160°C/gas mark 4.

Wrap each banana in foil, place directly onto an oven shelf and bake for 20 minutes.

Unwrap the hot roasted bananas and use a sharp knife to slice each one neatly in half along its length. Leaving the banana halves in their skins (they'll fall apart if you try to peel them now – just let people scoop out the flesh themselves as they eat), set two halves on each plate, sprinkle over some demerara sugar and serve with ice cream or, even better, lightly tangy frozen yoghurt.

Serves 4

4 ripe bananas, unpeeled

Demerara sugar, to sprinkle

Ice cream or frozen yoghurt,
   to serve

CINNAMON BANANA TEA LOAF

This banana bread doesn't use any added fat, but that's all in the name of texture – not health. With a leaner batter, this cake cooks to a slightly firmer texture, making it robust enough to be cut into thin slices, crisped lightly under the grill and smothered with salted butter and honey. It's also good in fatter chunks, nestled in packed lunch boxes and snaffled on the morning commute.

Preheat the oven to 180°C/fan 160°C/gas mark 4, and line the loaf tin with baking parchment.

Mash the bananas well in a large bowl before whisking in the sugar, eggs, milk and vanilla extract. Stir the dry ingredients together in a separate bowl before adding to the wet mix; beat until smooth. Pour the batter into the prepared tin and bake for 60–70 minutes, or until a knife or skewer sunk into the centre of the cake comes out with no more than a crumb or two stuck to it.

Leave to cool completely in its tin before unmoulding, slicing and serving.

Serves 6

2 medium bananas

125g dark muscovado sugar

2 large eggs

30ml milk

1 teaspoon vanilla extract

175g plain flour

2½ teaspoons baking powder

¼ teaspoon ground cinnamon

Generous pinch of salt

900g loaf tin

132

BANANA SESAME FRITTERS WITH BALSAMIC CARAMEL

These are the kind of no-fuss fritters you might find on the dessert menu of a Chinese restaurant or cheap buffet eatery; it's simple comfort food – deep-fried, sweet and moreish. You could use white sesame seeds but the black ones look better, contrasting with the golden batter. The simplest way to serve these is with a little warmed golden syrup, but here I've suggested a less sickly alternative: a sticky balsamic caramel sauce, with a slight acidity to take the edge off the sweetness.

There's more information on deep-frying on page 94 should you need it, but as long as you work slowly and carefully, and keep kids out of the kitchen, you should find it as easy as any other method of cooking. Make sure you chill the flour and water in advance as this will help the batter to puff on contact with the hot oil, for a light, crisp coating.

Combine the sugar and water for the caramel in a small pan (preferably not one with a non-stick coating) and set over a high heat. Apart from occasionally tilting the pan to very gently swirl the mixture, don't stir. Just let the syrup bubble until it has darkened to a deep amber colour. Immediately turn off the heat and pour in the cream and butter, whisking briskly to melt the butter through the hot caramel. Add the balsamic vinegar and salt to taste. Set aside while you prepare the banana fritters.

Pour the oil into a medium pan or deep fryer, taking care not fill it higher than two-thirds full. Heat the oil to 180°C, using a sugar thermometer to monitor the temperature if not using a deep fryer. In the 10–15 minutes that it'll take the oil to come up to temperature, prepare the fritter batter.

Combine the flour, caster sugar, baking powder, salt and sesame seeds together in a large bowl. Stir the water and egg yolks together in a separate bowl then pour half of this mixture into the dry ingredients, whisking continuously until smooth. Whisk in the remaining liquid, adding a little extra water if necessary, to give a thick, but not gloopy, batter.

Dip the banana pieces into the batter in batches, making sure they're completely covered, then place in the hot oil a few at a

Makes 25–30, enough for 6

For the balsamic caramel:
150g caster sugar
3 tablespoons water
110ml double cream
35g butter
1 tablespoon balsamic vinegar
Generous pinch of salt

For the fritters:
150g plain flour, chilled
50g caster sugar
1½ teaspoons baking powder
¼ teaspoon salt
40g black sesame seeds
175ml sparkling water, chilled
2 egg yolks
6–8 small ripe bananas, cut into 4cm chunks

1.5–2 litres vegetable or corn oil

time, depending on the size of your pan. They may sink to the bottom of the pan before rising back up to the surface – keep an eye on them and give them a nudge with a long-handled metal spoon if they stick to the base. Fry for 2 minutes, flip them, and cook for a further 2 minutes. If they stubbornly roll back over, bellies up, you might have to hold the fritters in place with a long-handled spoon to cook the second side. The fritters should be golden brown and sizzling after the 4 minutes. Remove with a slotted spoon and pat dry with kitchen paper. Keep the cooked fritters warm in a low oven while you fry the rest in batches, keeping the oil at 180–190°C all the while.

Serve the fritters with the balsamic caramel (rewarming it over a low heat if it's cooled and set) and generous scoops of vanilla ice cream.

WHITE CHOCOLATE AND PASSION FRUIT POTS

These pots are like little chocolate mousses, but with none of the hassle of whisking egg whites or setting with gelatine: just a passion fruit-laced white chocolate ganache, lightened with whipped cream. They need a couple of hours to set, but hands-on preparation time is minimal.

Halve the passion fruit and scoop the pulp into a sieve. Squeeze and press as much of the juice as possible into a small bowl and discard the seeds.

Heat the white chocolate and 4 tablespoons of the double cream in a heatproof bowl set over a pan of simmering water (making sure the bottom of the bowl doesn't touch the water). Once melted and silky smooth, add two-thirds of the passion fruit juice and stir in. Leave to cool to room temperature.

Whisk the remaining 90ml cream to soft peaks with 25g of the caster sugar, then gently fold this into the slightly cooled white chocolate and passion fruit mixture. Divide between the four ramekins or pudding basins and place in the fridge for two hours to set.

Once the chocolate pots are firm, make the topping. Mix the remaining 50g caster sugar and the cornflour, and heat this with the last third of the passion fruit juice in a small pan over a low heat, stirring continuously, until it has thickened to a syrupy consistency and is just about to boil. Leave to cool a little before pouring it over the chocolate pots. Place in the fridge again for 10–15 minutes then serve.

Makes 4

6 passion fruit

100g white chocolate, finely chopped

150ml double cream

75g caster sugar

1 teaspoon cornflour

Four ramekins or 150ml pudding basins

More recipes with tropical fruit:
Banana Thyme Cake with Lemon Glaze, page 98
Banana Crème Brûlée, page 215

CITRUS

ZESTY CHILLI PRAWN NOODLES

LEMON, BUTTERMILK AND
BLACK PEPPER CAKE

SUMMER ELDERFLOWER LIME TART

WARMING CHOCOLATE CHIP
JAFFA PUDDING

LEMON COURGETTE RISOTTO
WITH SUMMER HERBS

Zest has become a cliché in my cooking, somehow finding its way into everything from risotto to custard to stir fries and roasts. I won't stop, though, until the zester is forcibly prised from my grasping fingers. It's a spike of flavour that stands in contrast to whatever other warmth, savouriness, greenness or spice that forms the taste backdrop of your cooking. Just as in a photo or a painting or a film, where a pinprick detail or splash of colour can set a whole scene in motion, so here citrus brings a dish to life.

ZESTY CHILLI PRAWN NOODLES

This is where I'm at right now in the evolution of an old childhood favourite weeknight dinner – an orange-scented curry with bacon, tomatoes and madras that was designed to be served over pasta. This newer incarnation is just as sacrilegious in its mix of ingredients, I'm glad to say, and every bit as delicious, the lightness of the orange balancing rich coconut, tender noodles and the heat of fresh ginger.

Coconut cream is the stuff sold in small sachets or tetrapak cartons, and it's far thicker and creamier than standard coconut milk. If you've already got coconut milk in the cupboard, though, you can of course just use that: use half a can instead of the cream, and don't add any water.

Heat the oil in a medium pan over a low heat. Add the onion and cook for 10 minutes to soften, stirring occasionally, then add the garlic and ginger and fry for a further minute. Put a large pan of water on to boil.

When the garlic is fragrant and sizzling, add the curry paste (add more or less depending on how hot you want the noodles) and orange zest and cook for a further minute or two before pouring in the chopped tomatoes, coconut cream and water. Bring the mixture to a simmer, then leave to reduce over a low heat for 10 minutes. Add the mangetout and cook for a further 5 minutes.

While the curry simmers, cook the egg noodles for 3 minutes, or as instructed on the packet, in the pan of boiling water. Drain as soon as they're tender. Add the prawns to the curry and cook for a final 2–3 minutes, just enough to heat them through, then serve tossed through the cooked, drained noodles.

Serves 4

1 tablespoon vegetable oil

1 onion, finely chopped

3 cloves garlic, sliced

5cm fresh ginger, peeled and grated

1–2 tablespoons madras curry paste

Zest of 2 oranges

1 x 400g can chopped tomatoes

4 tablespoons coconut cream

100ml water

150g mangetout, trimmed

250g egg noodles

300g cooked and peeled king prawns

LEMON, BUTTERMILK AND BLACK PEPPER CAKE

This isn't just my favourite lemon drizzle cake but my new favourite cake, full stop. It's got all the sunny sharpness of a typical lemon cake, but with an added lightness and tang from the buttermilk, and a background heat from the coarsely ground black pepper. It's a heavenly trinity of flavours. Leave out the pepper if you're a traditionalist or if you want to ice this as a celebration cake. You could even swap the lemon for another citrus fruit: pink grapefruit works particularly well, and orange and lime pair nicely, too.

Preheat the oven to 180°C/fan 160°C/gas mark 4, and grease and line both cake tins.

Cream the butter with the sugars until light and fluffy then stir in the lemon zest, pepper and eggs. In a separate bowl, combine the flour, baking powder and salt and then add to the butter mixture along with the buttermilk. Stir until the batter is smooth.

Spoon the batter into the prepared tins and bake for 25 minutes, or until well-risen, golden brown and springy to the touch. Unmould the cakes and leave to cool on a wire rack.

Prepare the drizzle by heating the lemon juice and sugar together in a small pan and simmering for a minute or two. Pour over the cooling cake layers while the syrup is still hot.

To assemble the cake, spread one layer with the lemon curd and sandwich with the second half. You could pour on some zesty water icing to finish it off, if you like, but I prefer to keep it simple with just an extra grind of pepper and a sprinkling of finely grated lemon zest.

Serves 8–10

For the cake:

300g unsalted butter, softened

200g caster sugar

100g soft light brown sugar

Zest of 4 lemons

4 teaspoons coarsely ground black pepper

4 large eggs

300g plain flour

3½ teaspoons baking powder

Generous pinch of salt

100ml buttermilk or sour cream

For the drizzle:

Juice of 2 lemons

50g caster sugar

To fill and top:

150–200g lemon curd

Coarsely ground black pepper

1–2 teaspoons lemon zest

Two 20cm round spring-form or loose-bottomed cake tins

SUMMER ELDERFLOWER LIME TART

Elderflower adds a light floral edge to this sweet lime pie, shifting the simple sweet-sharpness into a more delicate balance. You'll need to give this tart at least a couple of hours to chill before serving, so make sure you leave yourself plenty of time. The flavours will actually meld and deepen the longer you leave it, so you could even make it the day before you plan to serve it.

Preheat the oven to 180°C/fan 160°C/gas mark 4.

Melt the butter in a pan over a low heat. Meanwhile, crush the digestive or hobnob biscuits to a very fine crumb, either in a food processor or in a freezer bag with a few good thwacks of the rolling pin. Mix the butter and crushed biscuits together then press into the base and 2–3cm up the sides of the cake tin. Pack the biscuit mixture firmly down with the back of a spoon. Bake for 10 minutes.

Whisk the condensed milk with the lime zest, lime juice and egg yolks for a couple of minutes, until thick and creamy, then stir in the elderflower cordial. Pour this mixture into the baked biscuit case and return to the oven for around 20 minutes, until just about set in the centre but still a little wobbly. Leave the tart to cool completely in its tin then transfer to the fridge to chill.

To make the topping, whisk the cream with the elderflower cordial until it holds soft peaks. Spoon over the chilled tart (or pipe it in patterns if you're feeling ambitious) then carefully run a knife around the edge of the biscuit crust and unmould the tart from its tin. Sprinkle a little extra lime zest over the top, then serve.

Serves 8

For the base:
110g butter
200g digestive or hobnob biscuits

For the filling:
400g condensed milk
Zest of 4–5 limes
125ml lime juice (from 4–5 limes)
3 large egg yolks
4 tablespoons elderflower cordial

For the topping:
225ml double cream
3 tablespoons elderflower cordial
Zest of 1 lime

20cm round spring-form cake tin

WARMING CHOCOLATE CHIP JAFFA PUDDING

This is a pudding that you could steam if you've got the time: follow the cooking instructions for the Chocolate Stout Pudding on page 357. Alternatively, if you want a quicker bake and a more cakey texture, cook in a 900g loaf tin, without the foil on top. It'll need less time in the oven, usually 35–45 minutes, so keep checking it until it's ready. Don't worry if it sinks in the middle – if it does, it's just because this is a very moist, soft cake.

Preheat the oven to 180°C/fan 160°C/gas mark 4. Grease the pudding basin and line the base with a circle of baking parchment. Have a couple of squares of kitchen foil to hand, ready to cover the pudding as it bakes.

Beat the butter, sugars, marmalade and orange zest together in a large bowl until smooth and light. Add the egg and milk and whisk to combine. In a separate bowl, stir together the flour, baking powder, nutmeg and salt, then add this to the wet ingredients and whisk until smooth. Fold in the chocolate chunks.

Spoon the batter into the prepared basin. Fold a wide pleat into the centre of each of the pieces of foil (this'll give the pudding room to rise), then layer them and place over the top of the pudding basin, folding neatly around the outside to secure. This foil hat will keep the steam as the pudding cooks. Bake in the preheated oven for 50 minutes, or until a small knife inserted into the middle of the pudding comes out more or less clean.

Serve with custard – better still a custard flecked with orange zest and a shot or two of whisky.

Serves 4–6

75g butter, softened

50g caster sugar

50g soft light brown sugar

4 tablespoons thick-cut marmalade

Zest of 1 orange

1 large egg

1 tablespoon milk

150g plain flour

1½ teaspoons baking powder

¼ teaspoon nutmeg

Pinch of salt

75g dark chocolate, chopped into small chunks

700ml pudding basin

LEMON COURGETTE RISOTTO WITH SUMMER HERBS

This summery risotto challenges the creamy heaviness of butter and Parmesan with plenty of lemon zest, courgette chunks and herbs, for a meal that's filling without being unpalatably rich. Risotto needs a lot of attention if it's going to develop that characteristic creaminess: constant stirring helps the rice to become starchy and sticky, and the liquid needs to be added gradually. That said, I quite like the catharsis that comes with this kind of hands-on cooking – by the time the risotto is ready you'll have an aching arm and a gleefully hearty appetite.

Preheat the oven to 180°C/fan 160°C/gas mark 4.

Spread the pine nuts over a baking tray and toast in the oven for 8–10 minutes, until lightly toasted and a shade or two darker. You can toast the nuts while the risotto's cooking if you prefer but they're prone to burning, so unless you're a good multitasker, I find it safest to get them done first.

Heat a little of the oil in a frying pan, dice two of the courgettes into cubes no bigger than 1cm or so across, and fry for 5 minutes until they're tender but still with some bite. Set aside to cool. Coarsely grate the remaining courgette.

In a large pan, heat the remaining oil then fry the spring onions for 2–3 minutes to soften. Add the risotto rice and stir to coat it in the oil, then pour in the wine and cook until almost all of the liquid has been absorbed and the alcohol has cooked off. Now for the hard graft: add the hot stock a ladleful at a time, stirring the risotto continuously at it cooks. As soon as most of the stock has been absorbed, it's time to add another ladleful, stir and repeat. After 15 minutes or so have passed, all of the stock should have been added and the rice should be creamy and thick.

Add the fried courgette cubes, grated courgette and lemon zest and cook for a further 2–3 minutes, then remove from the heat and beat in the butter, Parmesan and herbs. Serve immediately with a sprinkling of the toasted pine nuts on top of each portion.

Serves 4

3 tablespoons pine nuts
4 tablespoons olive oil
3 medium courgettes
4 spring onions, finely sliced
300g arborio risotto rice
125ml dry white wine
1.3–1.4 litres hot vegetable or chicken stock
Zest of 3 lemons
75g butter, chilled and diced
50g Parmesan, finely grated
Small handful each of basil, parsley and mint leaves, all finely chopped

146

More recipes with citrus fruit:

STONE FRUITS AND CHERRIES

HONEYED PLUM AND
PINE NUT CAKE

ZESTY LIME CHICKEN
WITH PEACH SALSA

SUMMER NECTARINE AND
GREEN BEAN SALAD WITH
MARINATED MOZZARELLA

ROASTED APRICOTS, ROSEMARY
FRANGIPANE AND MARSALA CREAM

CHERRY FETA BULGUR WHEAT
WITH TOASTED HAZELNUTS

I can trace my fondness for peaches back to wistful readings of *James and the Giant Peach* as a kid, and now that wonder sprawls across as far as smooth-skinned nectarines, runty plums and even insipid apricots. Each stone fruit is a potential giant peach, and every bite reminds me of the joy of the centipede, the ladybird and the grasshopper as they guzzle peach juice by the tankard, in grotesque, greedy glory.

Though I've grouped them together here, peaches, plums, nectarines, apricots and cherries could just as well have filled whole chapters by themselves: the burgundy blush, bitter skin and juicy flesh of a Victoria plum is worlds apart from the velvet-skinned, densely syrupy sweetness of a good, ripe peach. What they do have in common though is, of course, the stone in the middle. It's this stone (which, if you can be bothered to crack through to its kernel, tastes almondy and rich, but which can be toxic in bigger quantities) that gives these fruits their affinity with nuts and smooth vanilla, cream and custard. They work just as beautifully in more summery pairings too, though, particularly when you play up the latent acidity of peaches or apricots with a spritz of lemon or lime.

HONEYED PLUM AND PINE NUT CAKE

A dark, fragrant cake, sweet with honey and ripe autumn plums. Take care to use a good honey (I used an orange blossom one) because it will impart plenty of flavour, as well as sweetness. It makes a huge difference to the taste of the cake. I can't imagine anything being better suited to this than the unique punchiness of pine nuts, but you could swap in sunflower seeds or chopped almonds if you're after a cheaper alternative.

Preheat the oven 180°C/fan 160°C/gas mark 4 and grease the cake tin or oven dish. Cut the plums into segments (I cut mine into eights) and discard the stones.

Beat the butter and honey together in a large bowl until thick and creamy, then add the eggs one at a time. In a separate bowl, mix the flour, cinnamon, baking powder, bicarbonate of soda and salt before adding this dry mixture to the butter, honey and eggs, stirring well to combine. Add three-quarters of the pine nuts to the batter and fold in most of the plum segments.

Pour the mix into the prepared tin or oven dish and scatter the remaining pine nuts and plum pieces over the top. Bake for 45–50 minutes, until the cake is well risen and springy to the touch. Eat this while it's still warm from the oven, with a jug of hot vanilla custard.

Serves 8–10

5–6 ripe plums
  (roughly 400g)

125g butter, softened

175g runny honey

2 large eggs

225g plain flour

1 teaspoon ground cinnamon

1 teaspoon baking powder

½ teaspoon bicarbonate
  of soda

¼ teaspoon salt

100g pine nuts

20cm square cake tin
  or oven dish

ZESTY LIME CHICKEN WITH PEACH SALSA

Chicken breast is notoriously difficult to keep moist as it cooks, but a good few spoonfuls of lime-spiked peach salsa should help to remedy that. Though it would usually be tomato at the heart of a salsa, peachy sweetness is ideal for standing up to the punch of coriander, spring onion and lime. You can easily bring the chicken and salsa together in tacos or fajitas, perhaps with a little sliced avocado to fill out the meal.

Use a rolling pin to bash the chicken breast fillets between a couple of sheets of baking parchment, until the meat is slightly flattened (this will help it to cook evenly). Combine the chicken with the oil, garlic, lime zest, salt and cayenne pepper in a large freezer bag or plastic container, coating the chicken well with the marinade. Leave to rest in the fridge for at least 2 hours.

While the chicken marinates, prepare the salsa. Combine the peaches, tomatoes, spring onions, coriander, lime juice and oil in a large bowl, and season with plenty of salt.

Heat a heavy frying pan or griddle (no need to add oil, because the chicken will be lightly oiled already from its marinade). Fry the chicken over a medium heat for 5–8 minutes on each side, depending of the size of the breast fillets, until the juices run clear. Serve immediately with plenty of salsa.

Serves 4

For the chicken:

4 chicken breasts

4 tablespoons olive oil

4 cloves garlic, crushed

Zest of 3 limes

1 teaspoon salt

½ teaspoon cayenne pepper

Juice of 1 lime

For the salsa:

1 large or 2 medium peaches, diced

3 tomatoes, deseeded and chopped

2 spring onions, finely sliced

Couple of handfuls of fresh coriander, roughly chopped

Juice of 2 limes

2 tablespoons olive oil

Salt, to taste

SUMMER NECTARINE AND GREEN BEAN SALAD WITH MARINATED MOZZARELLA

This lemony summer salad is surprisingly filling, packed with ripe nectarines, salty-sweet Parma ham and the crunch of flaked almonds. Make sure you cook the green beans until they're perfectly tender: it's tempting to underdo them in the name of freshness, but truly there's nothing worse than beans that squeak between your teeth, so be thorough. Cheap mozzarella can be bland, but marinating it for a couple of hours with herbs, chilli, salt and oil will boost the flavour of even the most rubbery supermarket cheese.

Combine the mozzarella, dried oregano, dried mint, crushed chillies, salt and lemon peel in a small bowl and cover with the oil. Leave to marinate for at least 2 hours, but preferably overnight.

Trim the green beans and cook in boiling salted water for 5–6 minutes or until tender. Drain and leave to cool.

Cut the nectarines into slim segments and discard their stones. Whisk the lemon juice together with two tablespoons of the marinade oil and a little pepper to make a dressing. Drain the remaining marinade from the mozzarella (you can either just discard this excess oil or keep it for salad dressings). Toss the cooled green beans with the dressing then arrange on a serving plate with the nectarines, marinated mozzarella, Parma ham and flaked almonds. Scatter over the lemon zest before serving.

Serves 4

250g mozzarella, torn into chunks

2 teaspoons dried oregano

1 teaspoon dried mint

¼ teaspoon crushed chillies

¼ teaspoon salt

Rind of ½ lemon, peeled into strips

2 tablespoons olive oil

250g green beans, trimmed

3 ripe nectarines

Juice of ½ lemon

8 slices Parma ham, cut into thick ribbons

30g toasted flaked almonds*

Zest of 1 lemon, to serve

Pepper, to taste

* If you can't find these ready-toasted, just toast them yourself for 5–6 minutes in a 180°C/fan 160°C/gas mark 4 oven

ROASTED APRICOTS, ROSEMARY FRANGIPANE AND MARSALA CREAM

Unlike fuzzed peaches and dizzyingly fragrant summer nectarines, as sweet as nectar and heavy with sticky juice, apricots can be disappointing raw. They're slightly firmer and blander than their cousins, and a lot less fun. The best in apricots is unlocked when they're cooked – whether that's in a skillet with a glug of wine and a spoonful of sugar, planted into the batter of a light lemon cake or roasted, as in this elegant dessert, with almond frangipane and aromatic rosemary.

Preheat the oven to 200°C/fan 180°C/gas mark 6.

Halve the apricots, gently tease out their stones and arrange the halves cut side up on a baking tray. Beat the egg yolks, sugar, ground almonds, butter and salt together until smooth, and slip a scant teaspoon of this mixture into the hollow of each apricot half. Push a few needles of rosemary into each heap of frangipane, and scatter the filled apricots with a little extra demerara sugar. Bake for 10–12 minutes, until the flesh of the apricots is soft and yielding, and the frangipane golden brown.

While the apricots cook, whisk the double cream, icing sugar and marsala until the mixture holds soft peaks. Serve 3–4 apricot halves per person, with a generous dollop of sweet wine cream on the side.

Serves 4–5

8 ripe apricots

2 egg yolks

40g demerara sugar, plus 2 tablespoons for sprinkling

60g ground almonds

30g butter, softened

Pinch of salt

2–3 sprigs of rosemary

To serve:

150ml double cream

25g icing sugar

25ml marsala

CHERRY FETA BULGUR WHEAT WITH TOASTED HAZELNUTS

There can be a hesitance to bring sweet fruit into savoury cooking, but if you can set aside those anxieties for a while, you'll find that a freer hand with your ingredients goes a long way. Add a couple of ripe plums to a pan of braising pork chops, slip some apricot onto meaty kebab skewers or throw wedges of blushing fig over a thin-based pizza; let the sweetness of the fruit darken and caramelise or let it be a contrast to the earthy, salty or meaty flavours of a dish. Here, fresh summer cherries give life, colour and bite to a simple bulgur wheat salad. This is excellent with lamb kebabs, which work all the better for being marinated in a mixture of blitzed cherries, pomegranate molasses, garlic, oil and dried mint before they hit the grill. That said, you can also easily double the quantities to serve this as a vegetarian main course in its own right.

Add the bulgur wheat to boiling salted water and cook for 10–12 minutes, or until tender. Drain, add the olive oil and cinnamon, season generously and leave to cool.

While the bulgur wheat cools, toast the hazelnuts either in a 180°C/fan 160°C/gas mark 4 oven for 10 minutes or in a frying pan over a medium heat for a couple of minutes, turning frequently. They'll toast more evenly in the oven, but the stove-top method will do just fine if you don't feel like turning the oven on for this summery salad.

Stir the toasted nuts, prepared cherries, feta, red onion and parsley through the bulgur wheat and it's ready to serve.

Serves 4 as a side dish

125g bulgur wheat

1 tablespoon olive oil

¼ teaspoon ground cinnamon

75g blanched hazelnuts

200g dark cherries, quartered and stones removed

75g feta cheese, in 5mm cubes

½ red onion, finely chopped

Couple of fistfuls of parsley leaves, roughly chopped

Salt and black pepper, to taste

More recipes with stone fruits and cherries:
Cherry Maple Cakes with Goats' Cheese Cream, page 178
Coffee Cream Meringue with Cherries, page 345

BERRIES AND CURRANTS

GLAZED BLUEBERRY
FRITTER DOUGHNUTS

COCONUT RASPBERRY
RIPPLE ICE CREAM

BLACKCURRANT FOOL CAKE

ROASTED STRAWBERRY
CREAM PAVLOVAS

SALTED MILK CHOCOLATE
BLACKBERRY MOUSSE CAKE

HEDGEROW BOUNTY BUCKLE

Berries and currants are the queens of all fruit, I think, no matter their size. When I'm feeling at my most regal (and I hope this is a mindset that you too can channel whenever the confidence washes over you), I want only to recline with a stack of trashy magazines, *Keeping Up with the Kardashians* on TV and a veritable platter of jewel-like berries in front of me, to feast upon as I please.

No coincidence that I equate berries with luxury, though, when a flimsy punnet of ruby red raspberries costs as much as a diamond ring. There's a premium put on these tiny fruit, so it's well worth stockpiling and guzzling while they're in season, and enjoying cheaper frozen berries (they're just as good, save for strawberries, whose summery sweetness gets lost in translation in the freezer) for the rest of the year.

What makes many berries and currants so delightful to cook with is that they toe a fine line between sweet and sour. That acidity is what dances across your taste buds and means you're able to come back for one more, and another, and another, long after your stomach has filled. Raspberries, redcurrants and blackcurrants are particularly sharp, making them ideal against the backdrop of heavy, even claggy, dairy- and sugar-based dishes. Strawberries, meanwhile, might need that tartness played up with a splash of balsamic vinegar, orange or even a few chunks of rhubarb.

GLAZED BLUEBERRY FRITTER DOUGHNUTS

These fritters don't have the flashy good looks of glazed ring doughnuts, but I think there's something really endearing about their messiness, translucent with a butter glaze and mottled indigo with stains of bright blueberry juice. And because shaping is as simple as patting the dough flat and cutting it into rectangles, there's no fussy rolling out or pricey pastry cutters required. If you're nervous about deep-frying, turn to page 94 for a little more reassurance.

Stir together the flour, sugar, baking powder, bicarbonate of soda, salt, nutmeg and blueberries in a large bowl. Whisk together the eggs, milk and lemon zest in a separate jug or bowl, then pour into the dry ingredients. Gently stir together to get a rough, sticky dough, adding a splash more milk if necessary.

Pour the oil into a heavy-based pan, taking care not to fill the pan more than two-thirds full, and heat to 180°C. Monitor the temperature using a sugar thermometer, and don't leave the oil unattended. While the oil heats, prepare the glaze: stir together the icing sugar and water followed by the vanilla extract and melted butter.

Pat out the fritter dough on a well-floured surface until the dough is no thicker than the depth of the blueberries. It'll be quite wet and sticky, but that's exactly how it needs to be to rise well as it fries. Cut into 12 rectangles, re-rolling any scraps if necessary.

Fry in batches, taking care not to overcrowd the pan, for 1½–2 minutes on each side. Pat the doughnuts dry on a couple of sheets of kitchen paper then immediately dunk in the glaze. Let any excess glaze drip off and leave the fritter doughnuts to cool on a wire rack. Enjoy soon after cooking.

Makes 12

250g plain flour

50g caster sugar

2½ teaspoons baking powder

½ teaspoon bicarbonate of soda

¼ teaspoon salt

Pinch of nutmeg

200g blueberries

2 large eggs

60ml milk

Zest of 1 lemon

1–1.5 litres oil

To glaze:

250g icing sugar

60ml water

1½ teaspoons vanilla extract

50g unsalted butter, melted

COCONUT RASPBERRY RIPPLE ICE CREAM

This vegan coconut milk ice cream is a simpler alternative to the dairy-laden sort. As it isn't made with the usual custard base, it's a lot less intimidating than other ice cream recipes, and between the high fat content of the coconut milk and the generous dose of caster sugar, it doesn't set quite as solid as 'lighter' versions.

Whisk together the coconut milk, sugar, desiccated coconut, vanilla extract, cardamom seeds and lemon zest until well combined. Pour into a large, lidded container and place in the fridge for a couple of hours until well chilled.

While the coconut ice cream base chills, prepare the raspberry ripple mixture by heating the raspberries, sugar and lemon juice in a small pan for a few minutes until the raspberries sink into a mush and release their juices. Strain the mixture through a fine sieve to catch all the raspberry seeds then pour the liquid back into the pan. Whisk the cornflour with two tablespoons of cold water, stir quickly into the raspberry purée and heat until the mixture reaches the boil. Remove from the heat and leave to cool completely, then scoop into a clean bowl and move to the fridge to chill.

Transfer the chilled coconut ice cream base to the freezer and whisk vigorously at 45-minute intervals until the ice cream is very thick and almost completely frozen. When you get to this point swirl through the raspberry purée, taking care not to over-mix, or you'll lose that sharp contrast between fruit and ice cream. Return the rippled ice cream to the freezer to set completely (a further hour or so). You might need to soften the ice cream at room temperature for 10–15 minutes before serving.

Makes 1 litre

2 x 400ml cans coconut milk

250g caster sugar

100g desiccated coconut

1½ tablespoons vanilla extract

Seeds from 8 cardamom pods, finely crushed

Zest of 2 lemons

For the raspberry ripple:

350g raspberries

60g caster sugar

Juice of 1 lemon

2 tablespoons cornflour

BLACKCURRANT FOOL CAKE

The perfect fool is a careful balancing act: the tartness of the fruit pitted against the smooth sweetness of the softly whipped cream. The best ones use fruits with a natural acidity to them, stepping away from the so-so niceness of strawberries and towards gooseberries, fresh currants and rhubarb, yielding a dessert that can jump from sweet, to mellow, to milky, to wincingly sharp all in one mouthful. This cake, sandwiching layers of soft, syrup-stained almond sponge with currants and cream, is a more substantial twist on that perfect fool.

Preheat the oven to 180°C/fan 160°C/gas mark 4. Grease and line the tins with baking parchment.

Beat the butter with the sugar until light and fluffy, then whisk in the eggs one at a time, followed by the ground almonds and lemon zest. In a separate bowl, stir the flour, baking powder, bicarbonate of soda and salt together, then add this to the wet ingredients. Fold everything together until just about combined, then divide between the three tins (if you only have two tins, just reserve a third of the mixture and bake it afterwards – the wait won't harm it).

Bake the cakes for around 15 minutes, or until risen and golden – a small knife inserted into the centre of each cake should emerge clean. Leave the cake layers to cool before unmoulding.

While the cakes cook and cool, you can make the syrup. Simmer the blackcurrants, caster sugar, water and lemon juice together for 3–5 minutes, then press through a fine sieve, collecting the juice and pulp while leaving the currant skins and stalks behind. Whisk the double cream and sugar together until thick enough to hold soft peaks.

Drizzle a couple of tablespoons of syrup over each sponge. Spread a third of the cream over one sponge, scatter over a third of the uncooked blackcurrants, add some mint and drizzle over a tablespoon of syrup. Repeat twice to use the remaining cake layers, cream, blackcurrants, mint and syrup. Serve immediately.

Serves 8–10

175g unsalted butter, softened

175g caster sugar

3 large eggs

50g ground almonds

Zest of 1 lemon

175g plain flour

1½ teaspoons baking powder

½ teaspoon bicarbonate of soda

Generous pinch of salt

For the syrup:

150g blackcurrants

75g caster sugar

60ml water

Juice of ½ lemon

To assemble:

300ml double cream

3 tablespoons caster sugar

100g blackcurrants

A few fresh mint leaves, torn

Three 20cm round spring-form or loose-bottomed cake tins

ROASTED STRAWBERRY CREAM PAVLOVAS

For years I refused to expose strawberries to even the slightest breath of warm air, so convinced was I by those who preached that strawberries are best when they're raw, at their purest. Those years were wasted ones, and those people were wrong: a punnet of perfectly ripe, deep-red, dimpled strawberries is a beautiful thing, and certainly not something to fuss and tamper with; but standard supermarket strawberries – washed out and mottled with green – can only benefit from a little heat. Roast strawberries with a few spoonfuls of sugar and a drop of balsamic vinegar and any unripe insipidity melts into glorious dark, sticky sweetness, perfect on top of a dollop of softly whipped, sweetened cream and crumbling meringue.

I've given instructions here on the assumption that you'll be using an electric hand whisk, just because meringues are so much easier if you have that extra bit of power on your side. But you can certainly make these the old-fashioned way if you don't have an electric whisk or mixer – just be prepared to have to flex your arm muscles and to whisk for at least 10–15 minutes to get a thick, glossy meringue.

Preheat the oven to 150°C/fan 130°C/gas mark 2 and line a large baking tray with baking parchment.

In a very clean bowl (preferably glass or metal, as these retain less grease than plastic ones), whisk the egg whites until densely foamy. Add the sugar a quarter at a time, whisking on high speed for a good 30 seconds between each addition. Once all the sugar has been incorporated, continue to whisk for 5–8 minutes, or until the meringue mixture is glossy, very thick and no longer grainy. It's ready when it holds a stiff, perfectly upright peak when you slowly lift the whisk from the mixture.

Spoon the meringue into eight mounds on the parchment-lined baking sheet and pat each meringue gently down to a disc shape no more than 2–3cm thick, scooping a slight hollow at its centre. Bake for 1 hour until the meringues are risen, crisp and set, with dry bottoms.

Makes 6 mini pavlovas
2 large egg whites
120g caster sugar

For the strawberries:
600g strawberries
60g caster sugar
1½ tablespoons balsamic vinegar

For the cream:
225ml double cream
30g caster sugar

Leave the meringues to cool while you turn the oven temperature up to 180°C/fan 160°C/gas mark 4 and prepare the strawberries. Rinse the fruit, remove any leaves and quarter or halve them, depending on their size. Toss them with the caster sugar and spread over a large baking tray or oven dish. Drizzle over the balsamic vinegar and roast for 20 minutes, or until the juices are bubbling and syrupy, and the strawberries are meltingly soft.

While the strawberries roast, whip the cream with the sugar until smooth and thick enough to spoon in generous dollops. Heap each pavlova with hot strawberries and cool cream, and eat straight away.

SALTED MILK CHOCOLATE BLACKBERRY MOUSSE CAKE

This mousse cake isn't the intensely dark sort but a lighter version made with mild milk chocolate and the odd fruity pop of blackberry. You can swap the blackberries for raspberries if the troublesome blackberry seeds frustrate you against the quivering smoothness of the cake.

Preheat the oven to 180°C/fan 160°C/gas mark 4. Grease the cake tin and line the base with baking parchment.

In a large bowl set over a pan of simmering water, or in the microwave on low, melt the chocolate and butter together. Leave to cool for 5 minutes before whisking in the egg yolks and vanilla extract.

Set the egg whites aside in a large, very clean glass or metal bowl then use an electric mixer to whisk until thick and foamy. Add the sugar a quarter at a time, whisking on high speed between each addition until the egg-sugar mixture holds stiff peaks.

Stir a third of the whisked egg whites into the chocolate mixture before gently folding in the rest until just combined, and still lightly marbled. In a separate bowl, combine the flour, cocoa powder and salt, then sift it into the egg mixture, folding everything lightly together. As soon as the batter is smooth, scatter the blackberries onto the base of the prepared tin and softly dollop the aerated batter on top.

Bake for 30–35 minutes, until well risen and just barely set. Watch the cake sink and crumple as it cools to a sticky, mousse-like finish.

Serves 8

100g milk chocolate, finely chopped

100g salted butter

3 large eggs, separated

1 teaspoon vanilla extract

125g caster sugar

35g plain flour

2 tablespoons cocoa powder

Good pinch of salt

200g blackberries

20cm round spring-form cake tin

HEDGEROW BOUNTY BUCKLE

A buckle is an American pudding cake filled with seasonal fruit and given a buttery crumble topping. Blueberries are traditional, and my favourite, but you can use whatever mixture of currants or berries happen to be in your fridge, on the shelves or decorating the hedgerows at the time: think redcurrants and blackcurrants, blackberries, raspberries and sweet red gooseberries. Just be sure to halve any larger berries, and add a little more sugar if you're using sharp currants or early green gooseberries.

I've used brown butter in this recipe because its nuttiness really complements the fruit and spice. In brown butter – made by simmering butter until it darkens a shade – the fatty blandness of normal butter is displaced and a richer flavour takes its place. It's a great cheat to bear in mind if ever you want to play up autumnal, caramelised or nutty notes in your baking.

Preheat the oven to 180°C/fan 160°C/gas mark 4. Grease the cake tin and line the base with a circle of baking parchment.

Cube the butter and set it in a small, heavy-based pan over a medium heat. Let the butter melt then watch it carefully as it simmers. Whisk the pan off the heat as soon as it begins to smell nutty and tiny flecks of brown begin to colour at the bottom of the pan. Decant the butter – including as much of the brown sediment as possible – into a clean bowl to cool a little.

Combine two-thirds of the now just-warm butter with the sugar, eggs, sour cream and vanilla extract in a large mixing bowl. Whisk together until thick and smooth. In a separate bowl, combine the flour, baking powder and grated nutmeg, then add to the wet mixture and fold together for a glossy, yellow batter. Gently stir in the berries and/or currants.

For the crumble topping, combine the flour, sugar and cinnamon in a bowl, then pour in the remaining third of brown butter. Rub everything together between your fingertips until it holds together in small clumps.

Spoon the berry-studded batter into the prepared cake tin and scatter the crumble clumps all over the top. Bake for around 1 hour, keeping the oven door firmly shut for the first 45 minutes.

Serves 12

150g salted butter

150g caster sugar

2 large eggs

150g sour cream

1½ teaspoons vanilla extract

250g plain flour

3 teaspoons baking powder

½ teaspoon grated nutmeg

300g berries and currants

For the cinnamon crumble topping:

75g plain flour

50g caster sugar

¼ teaspoon ground cinnamon

20cm round spring-form cake tin

Thanks to the insulating layer of the crumble topping, this cake rises incredibly well considering the amount of fruit weighing it down. The topping traps in a little of the steam and protects the surface from the direct heat of the oven, meaning it sets more slowly – and so rises more – than it might otherwise.

Test to see whether the cake is cooked: a small knife inserted into the middle should emerge with little more than a crumb or two stuck to it. Remove from the tin and serve while it's still warm.

More recipes with berries and currants:
Pink Lemonade Crush with Mint, page 99
Pear, Blackberry and Coconut Cake, page 120
Orange Blossom Panna Cotta with Strawberries, page 209
Blueberry Cheesecake Swirl Ice Cream, page 214
Meatballs with Sticky Blackberry-anise Sauce, page 265
Blueberry Yoghurt Loaf Cake, page 336

EGGS
AND
DAIRY

CHEESE

CHERRY MAPLE CAKES WITH
GOATS' CHEESE CREAM

BEETROOT AND FETA FILO CIGARS

PERFECT GRILLED CHEESE
SANDWICHES WITH QUICK
PICKLED CUCUMBER

FRIED GOATS' CHEESE WITH
THYME AND HONEY

BROOKLYN CHEESECAKE

So much cheese finds its way into my cooking – on pasta and in pies, stirred through everything from soups to stews and even savoury crumble toppings – but even more gets lost en route: a slice or six of Red Leicester nibbled beside the stove, a crystalline chunk of good, aged Gruyère pilfered from the chopping board, even a honey-drizzled morsel of goats' cheese. If you look in my fridge on any given day, there's a good chance you'll find half a block of tooth-marked Cheddar guiltily tucked into the door.

And yet, in spite of my habit, I've never really made an effort to learn about the cheese I eat, much less to actually let it shine. Too often cheese is an afterthought when I cook, thrown in for richness or for seasoning, but rarely as an important ingredient in its own right. The recipes in this chapter are an attempt to do better.

That's not to say that I'm ready to be a cheese connoisseur, though, and as long as I live I'll never choose a cheeseboard over a dessert. I'm still here for all of you who eat cheese spread from a squeezy pack, snack on cheesestrings in the streets and Babybel in bed. There's no hierarchy here, just as much cheese as possible, in as many permutations and combinations as you can think of.

CHERRY MAPLE CAKES WITH GOATS' CHEESE CREAM

I've always had a special fondness for cheese with fruit: not the traditional marriages of apple and Cheddar or pear and Gorgonzola, but the brasher, brighter mix of jam and cheese. I love the salt-sweet confusion of cheese and jam sandwiches, and the fact that it's anathema to whoever has to share a lunch table with me only thrills me more. Here's a gentler match along those lines – cherry jam with mild goats' cheese, pulled together in the form of little cakes. Because the tang of the goats' cheese is subdued with extra cream and syrup, you shouldn't find it too jarring at all, even if goats' cheese isn't typically your thing.

Preheat the oven to 180°C/fan 160°C/gas mark 4. Line the muffin tin with paper muffin cases.

In a large bowl, beat the butter with the brown sugar until light and fluffy, then stir in the maple syrup and almond extract. One at a time, add the eggs. Measure the flour, ground almonds, baking powder and salt into the mixing bowl and stir everything together just until the batter is smooth and well combined.

Divide the batter between the muffin cases, then dollop a scant teaspoon of cherry jam into the middle of each (it should sink down as the cakes cook). Bake for 25 minutes or so, until well risen and set through. Brush a teaspoon of maple syrup over the top of each cake, then leave to cool in the tin.

While the muffins cool, prepare the goats' cheese cream. Beat the cheese with the maple syrup until perfectly smooth. Separately, whisk 150ml of the double cream to soft peaks (take care not to over-whip it or it'll become grainy) then stir a small amount into the sweetened goats' cheese to slacken it. Gently fold the remaining whipped cream into the goats' cheese mixture. Whip and add the remaining 75ml double cream for a milder flavour, if you want.

Serve the cakes with a spoonful of goats' cheese cream on the side. You can ice them properly if you prefer, smoothing a thick layer of cream over the top of each cake as you would a buttercream, but it's harder work and you'll have to keep the cakes in the fridge afterwards, thanks to the whipped cream.

Makes 12

150g unsalted butter, softened

100g soft light brown sugar

4 tablespoons maple syrup, plus extra for brushing

¼ teaspoon almond extract

2 large eggs

125g plain flour

100g ground almonds

2 teaspoons baking powder

Pinch of salt

125g cherry jam

For the cream:

150g soft, mild goats' cheese

2 tablespoons maple syrup

150–225ml double cream

12-hole muffin tin

BEETROOT AND FETA FILO CIGARS

I've taken inspiration from Turkish *börek*, wrapping cheese in tissue-thin layers of filo pastry, though my cigars are very different from the authentic versions. I've mixed grated beetroot and pistachios through the basic feta cheese filling, complementing the briny clout of the cheese with something a little milder and sweeter, but you can play around with different flavour combinations however you'd like. A good handful of parsley would work well, as would a few chopped olives, a little dill and even some wilted spinach. I know it doesn't compare in terms of flavour, but pre-grated mozzarella is better in this recipe than fresh mozzarella grated at home: it's far drier and firmer, allowing a crisper finish on the pastry.

Melt the butter, coarsely grate the beetroot, crumble the feta into small chunks and finely chop the pistachios.

Lay a sheet of filo out with one of the short edges nearest to you and brush it all over with the melted butter. (Keep the rest of the filo covered, preferably with a moistened cloth, while you work, or it'll dry and become brittle.) Scatter some of the feta, mozzarella, beetroot and pistachio in a line across the width of the filo sheet, at the end nearest to you, stopping just short of the edges. Roll the filling up inside the filo to give a cigar-shaped pastry. Brush the outside with more melted butter. Set the filo parcel to one side while you make two or three more, or as many as you can fit in the frying pan at once.

Cook on a medium-low heat for 5 minutes on each side, until both top and bottom are a rich brown colour, and the filling is piping hot. If the pastries stick you can brush the pan with a little oil, but the butter over the filo should suffice to prevent this. Repeat the filling, rolling and cooking until you've made all twelve pastries. Enjoy while hot, either as a fun veggie main, with a grain salad and greens, or by themselves as a snack.

Makes 12

100g butter

300g cooked beetroot

300g feta cheese

100g pistachios

12 sheets filo pastry, each roughly 25x30cm

100g grated mozzarella

PERFECT GRILLED CHEESE SANDWICHES WITH QUICK PICKLED CUCUMBER

There's no mystery to a good grilled cheese sandwich, but it needs a little care. The best I ever had was a modest sandwich in a Brooklyn diner, served unpromisingly on a chipped white plate with a greasy napkin, a sad-looking gherkin on the side: the bread was just thick enough to develop a greasy, golden crust, just cheap and thin enough not to overwhelm the cheese; the filling was a mixture of cheeses – a milder, melting cheese and a second sharper one to cut through the gooey richness. This recipe is an attempt to recreate that bliss, though you should feel free to swap in your favourite cheeses and condiments as you please.

These are best made in a cast-iron pan, though any heavy pan will do. If your frying pan is very thin, take extra care and cook on a very low heat to avoid burning the bread before the cheese has had a chance to melt.

Slice the cucumber into very fine rounds, toss together with the salt then leave to sit for 15 minutes.

Heat a little oil in a large, heavy-based frying pan over a medium-low heat. Set a couple of the slices of bread in the pan, heap them with plenty of Gruyère and Gouda and sprinkle with just a pinch of cayenne. Top each one with another slice of bread and weigh each sandwich down with a heavy plate, or press down under a grill weight. Fry for 3 minutes or so until the underneath is browned but not burnt, then flip and cook the other side for a further 3–4 minutes, leaving the cheese molten and the outside greasily crisp. Add a drop more oil to the pan before repeating with the remaining bread and cheese.

In the stolen minutes you can find while the sandwiches cook, prepare the quick cucumber pickle. Drain any liquid from the salted cucumber (the salt should have drawn out some of its moisture) and combine with the vinegar, sugar, mustard and dill.

Serve each sandwich hot from the pan with a good spoonful of pickled cucumber on the side or, for a zero-prep accompaniment, some red onion rings, jalapeño, finely sliced radishes or gherkin.

Serves 4

½ cucumber

¼ teaspoon salt

Vegetable oil, for frying

8 slices light rye or sourdough bread

150g Gruyère, grated

150g Gouda, grated

Pinch of cayenne pepper

1½ tablespoons white wine vinegar

2 teaspoons caster sugar

½ teaspoon wholegrain mustard

1 dill frond, finely chopped

FRIED GOATS' CHEESE WITH THYME AND HONEY

In essence, these bites are a more refined version of the mozzarella dippers I spent my formative years eating from grease-soaked paper bags in chip shops and pizza joints. They're not necessarily better than fast-food versions (there's still a special place in my heart for the salty blandness of those dippers, designed to be bolstered with the acid kick of a chilli tomato sauce, and food needs to be immune to those loaded value judgements that come with making it 'fancy'), but where these goats' cheese bites pull apart from their chip-shop cousins is in their subtlety. The goats' cheese imparts a slight tang, complemented by the flavour of the thyme in a breadcrumb coating. You don't have to serve these with honey if you don't think it has a place in a savoury snack, but give it a try and you'll find that the sweetness accents the delicate flavour of the cheese.

Cut the goats' cheese block into long batons no thicker than 1cm wide, wrap in cling film and place in the freezer for 20–30 minutes. Freezing will help the cheese to cook evenly and keep its shape, stopping it from just collapsing straight into a sticky mess the second it hits the hot oil.

Prepare three wide bowls or plates: the first containing the flour, the second the beaten egg, and the third the breadcrumbs, thyme and lemon zest, well seasoned with salt and pepper. Heat the oil in a heavy-based, non-stick frying pan.

Once the goats' cheese sticks are cold, dip them one by one in the flour, then egg, then breadcrumbs in turn, working quickly between the second and third dishes to avoid the egg freezing onto the cold cheese. Add the breadcrumb-coated goats' cheese in batches to the hot oil (it ought to be hot enough to sizzle as soon as the cheese hits it) and cook over a medium heat for 30 seconds. Turn the cheese sticks over and cook for a further 30 seconds, repeating for each of the four long edges. If the breadcrumbs brown too quickly or not at all, adjust the heat accordingly. Pat dry on a couple of sheets of kitchen paper then serve straight away drizzled with a little honey.

Makes 12 goats' cheese bites

250g firm goats' cheese, such as St Helen's

50g plain flour

1 egg, lightly beaten

50g panko breadcrumbs

1 tablespoon dried thyme

Zest of ½ lemon

100–150ml light olive oil, for frying

Salt and black pepper, to taste

75g runny honey, to serve

BROOKLYN CHEESECAKE

A slice of cheesecake might have been my first real love. I bought it in the same Brooklyn diner that inspired the grilled cheese sandwich in the recipe on page 182, and carried it back to my room many blocks away in −15°C weather, cradling it to me to keep it warm. As soon as the bedroom door clicked shut behind me, I took a plastic fork to it and ate the whole thing in just a few greedy mouthfuls. It was a lonely time in New York and I'd been cold for days, and that velvety smooth cheesecake made my frozen fingers, wet socks and all of the aching tiredness worthwhile and for a few minutes at least, I felt at home. If I could fly, I'd go right back to where I bought that cheesecake; I'd give up as much as the cashier asked me to. For your eyes only, here's my best shot at recreating that piece of joy.

Preheat the oven to 180°C/fan 160°C/gas mark 4. Get the ingredients out of the fridge, where applicable, to come to room temperature before assembling: it'll make it a lot easier to get a smooth cheesecake batter.

Crush the digestive biscuits, either in a food processor or just by bashing them with a rolling pin, until they're reduced to a powdery rubble, with no chunks left. Melt the butter then mix with the crushed biscuits in a bowl. Pack the buttery biscuit mixture into the base of the cake tin, pushing it firmly down under the bottom of a glass or spoon. Bake the biscuit base for 10–12 minutes, then leave to cool and reduce the oven temperature to 130°C/fan 110°C/gas mark ½–1.

Beat the cream cheese in a mixing bowl until perfectly smooth. In a separate bowl, mix the caster sugar and cornflour together before stirring into the cream cheese then crack in the eggs, one at a time, and stir in. Finally, pour in the double cream and vanilla extract and whisk lightly, taking care not to incorporate any air (it's a dense, smooth texture we're after here), until everything is combined.

Pour the cheesecake mixture over the baked base and transfer to the oven to cook for 1–1¼ hours, or until the cheesecake is just barely set – there should still be the slightest jiggle at its centre, but it should be set and barely puffed around the edges. As soon as it's ready, run a knife around the edge to loosen it from

Serves 12

175g digestive biscuits

90g salted butter

600g full-fat cream cheese

200g caster sugar

2 tablespoons cornflour

3 large eggs

150ml double cream

1 tablespoon vanilla extract

20cm round spring-form cake tin

the tin (this should stop it cracking as it cools and shrinks) and leave to cool completely in the tin. Transfer to the fridge and let the cheesecake chill for at least 3–4 hours before serving, but preferably a full 48 hours if you have the discipline, to let the texture settle into fudgy smoothness and the flavour develop that trademark tang.

More recipes with cheese:
15-minute Herb-crusted Grilled Aubergine, page 29
Courgette, Mint and Ricotta Fritters, page 34
Charred Asparagus with Dukkah, Feta and Hazelnut Oil, page 40
Kale, Sweet Potato and Mozzarella Pie, page 49
Mushroom and Mozzarella Braided Loaf, page 60
Pearl Barley, Mushroom and Taleggio Risotto, page 62
Hot Beetroot, Hazelnuts and Goats' Cheese, page 70
Carrot and Feta Bites with Lime Yoghurt, page 73
Sweet Potato, Feta and Pumpkin Seed Muffins, page 89
Two-potato Dauphinoise, page 91
Cheddar Crust Apple Pie, page 113
Summer Nectarine and Green Bean Salad with Marinated Mozzarella, page 154
Cherry Feta Bulgur Wheat with Toasted Hazelnuts, page 157
Mystic Pizza, page 201
Herbed Salmon and Ricotta Quiche, page 203
Blueberry Cheesecake Swirl Ice Cream, page 214
Cider-spiked Fish Pie, page 274
Sticky Walnut Cinnamon Swirls, page 305

EGGS

SHAKSHUKA

CHILLI CORNBREAD PANCAKES

ROASTED GARLIC, MUSHROOM
AND GOATS' CHEESE FRITTATA
WITH CRISP RADISH SALAD

HARRY STYLES'S DUTCH BABY
WITH CINNAMON RHUBARB

MYSTIC PIZZA

HERBED SALMON AND
RICOTTA QUICHE

There's a quote from American food writer M.F.K. Fisher that might be my favourite sentence: 'Probably one of the most private things in the world is an egg before it is broken.' You can try to get a feel for an egg, testing its weight in the palm of your hand, floating it in water, pricking your ears to the slosh or silence as you shake it, but the only way to ever really know it is to break it. All the secrets an egg can hold: it can be a slick of translucent white and a golden yolk, whip up to twice its size, set rubbery or silkily smooth, rise to towering peaks or fall into a sulphurous slump.

People can be so fussy about the right and wrong ways to cook eggs, but I'm not here to wade in on those tired debates. If your perfect omelette is as tough as leather and packed full of cheap cheese, that's fine by me; if your secret for poached eggs is laced with magic, ritual and charm, then keep doing what you do. I can't reinvent the egg, but I can share with you a few of my favourite recipes – ones where eggs don't just fill, bind, glaze, foam or rise, but take centre stage with their secrets.

SHAKSHUKA

Each meal is a chance to try something new, to nourish and be good to yourself, and in that spirit I'm very much of the belief that we should honour every mealtime with equal reverence. Breakfast isn't necessarily the most important meal of the day – we owe it to ourselves to dismiss these rules wherever we can. But a good breakfast does set the tone for the day, so it's well worth taking the time to indulge if you can. Here's the breakfast I cook on sluggish weekend mornings to give me the energy and resolve to tide me through a whole day of doing sweet nothing. It's a North African dish originally, but I've served it with spicy cornbread pancakes (see opposite) to shake things up.

Heat the oil in a large frying pan (a heavy cast-iron one is best for this, but anything will do as long as it's not too shallow). Fry the cumin seeds over a high heat for a minute until they start to sizzle, then turn the heat down and add the onion, garlic and spices. Cook for 2 minutes before adding the diced peppers. Let the vegetables soften for 10 minutes before adding the tomato purée, chopped tomatoes and enough boiling water to just cover everything.

Leave to simmer, uncovered, for 10 minutes then season well and add a splash more water if you have to. Set the heat low enough that the sauce is barely bubbling, then make four little hollows in the pepper mixture and crack the eggs into them, spacing them well apart. Cover the pan with a lid and leave to cook gently for 6–8 minutes, until the eggs are perfectly poached. Sprinkle with the chopped parsley and spring onion.

Serves 4

3 tablespoons olive oil
1 teaspoon cumin seeds
1 onion, diced
1 clove garlic, thinly sliced
1 teaspoon smoked paprika
¼ teaspoon chilli flakes
Pinch of cayenne pepper
2 red peppers, diced
2 green peppers, diced
1 tablespoon tomato purée
1 x 400g can chopped
  tomatoes
250–350ml boiling water
4 eggs
Handful of chopped parsley
  and finely sliced spring
  onion, to top
Salt and black pepper,
  to taste

CHILLI CORNBREAD PANCAKES

Serve these pancakes with the Shakshuka (see opposite), or nudge them from brunch into lunch by serving with a bowl of hot chilli con carne.

Stir the dry ingredients and chillies together in a large bowl then whisk in the buttermilk or milk, and the eggs. Leave the batter to sit for 10 minutes then add extra milk if it needs it – enough to give a thick, just-pourable consistency.

Heat a little oil in a large heavy-based frying pan over a medium-low heat and for each cornbread pancake dollop a tablespoon or two of the batter into the pan, using just enough to make circles roughly the size of scotch pancakes. Cook them in batches for 1½–2 minutes on each side, adjusting the temperature as necessary to give a golden brown – not charred – crust on each side. These are best eaten warm, so keep cooked ones toasty in a low-temperature oven while you work.

Makes 12–14 small pancakes, serving 4

250g instant polenta

1 tablespoon caster or soft light brown sugar

2½ teaspoons baking powder

¼ teaspoon salt

2 green chillies, deseeded and finely chopped

400–600ml buttermilk or milk

2 large eggs

Vegetable oil, for frying

ROASTED GARLIC, MUSHROOM AND GOATS' CHEESE FRITTATA WITH CRISP RADISH SALAD

Roasting garlic strips it of its ascetic, pungent sharpness and leaves it sweet, mellow and soft. It's a far rounder flavour – perfect for adding a little depth to this herby, mushroom-laden frittata. If you're really pressed for time, though, you can use unroasted garlic instead: add one finely sliced clove for this amount of egg, frying it for a minute once the onion has softened.

This makes far more roasted garlic than you'll need for this frittata, but that needn't go to waste. Try whisking it in to vinaigrettes, tossing through linguine with plenty of chilli oil or even stuffed under chicken skin before a roast.

To roast the garlic, preheat the oven to 200°C/fan 180°C/gas mark 6. Cut the top off of the bulb, slicing clean through the upper 5mm or so of the cloves, leaving their tops exposed. Peel away all the excess papery skin from the outside, leaving just the skin of the individual cloves and the root section holding them all in place. Place on a sheet of kitchen foil, drizzle half of the oil over the top of the bulb and wrap tightly into a foil package. Roast for 1 hour, until the cloves are so soft they melt at the press of a finger. Leave to cool.

In a small, heavy-based pan (preferably a cast-iron one), heat the remaining tablespoon of oil and fry the shallots or onion on a low heat for 5 minutes, to soften slightly. Crush in 2 cloves of the roasted garlic (you can leave the skins on as you squeeze the soft flesh through a garlic crusher), add the thyme leaves and cook for another minute, stirring all the time. Add the mushrooms and fry for 10–15 minutes over a medium-low heat, stirring often, until they have softened and released their juices, and most of that liquid has bubbled away.

While the mushrooms cook, preheat the grill to high and prepare the salad: very finely slice the radishes and carrot then toss with the thyme leaves, olive oil and white wine vinegar, and season with plenty of salt and pepper.

Serves 2

1 whole garlic bulb

2 tablespoons olive oil

2 shallots or ½ onion, finely sliced

Leaves from 3–4 sprigs of thyme

125g chestnut or portobello mushrooms, sliced

4 large eggs

3 tablespoons milk

75g soft goats' cheese, in chunks or slices

Salt and black pepper, to taste

For the radish salad:

8 radishes, topped and tailed

1 carrot

Leaves from 2 sprigs of thyme

1 tablespoon olive oil

1 teaspoon white wine vinegar

Salt and black pepper, to taste

Whisk the eggs and milk together and season generously with salt and pepper. Take the pan off the heat and pour the eggs into the pan over the cooked mushrooms, shaking the pan a couple of times to just roughly combine everything. Scatter over the goats' cheese and return the pan to the hob, cooking over a medium-low heat for 3–4 minutes. Don't stir the frittata mixture at all while it cooks, or you'll end up with scrambled eggs.

Once the bottom has had a few minutes to set, transfer the pan to the grill and cook the top for a further 3–4 minutes, until the egg is barely quivering at the centre. Resist the temptation to cook it to a golden brown finish, or the egg will become rubbery and tough. Serve straight away with the radish salad.

HARRY STYLES'S DUTCH BABY WITH CINNAMON RHUBARB

Harry Styles once recommended a version of this dessert to my friend's dad while sitting at the counter of Soho restaurant Spuntino – that was all the incentive I needed to come up with a recipe of my own. A Dutch Baby sits somewhere between a Yorkshire pudding and a pancake: a sweet, cinnamon-spiced batter, blasted in a hot oven until it rises to airy perfection. Served with tart rhubarb and ice cream, it's a great dessert, though you could tone down the sweetness and just heap it with fresh berries for a fine breakfast, too. I don't always have time to treat myself to this indulgent brunch treat, but through all the muesli and porridge and sad cereal bars, it's this little baby that I miss.

Put the rhubarb, sugar, cinnamon and star anise in a pan and cook over a low heat for 10–15 minutes. The rhubarb will start off defiantly crunchy, but as it warms it will soften and release its juices until you're left with a rosy rhubarb compote.

Preheat the oven to 200°C/fan 180°C/gas mark 6. Have a 17–20cm cast-iron frying pan or similar size pie dish to hand.

In a mixing bowl, whisk the sugar, eggs and milk together. Combine the flour, cinnamon, nutmeg and salt in a separate bowl. Add a little of the egg mixture to the dry ingredients and whisk to a thick paste before pouring in the remaining liquid. Mix the batter until smooth, then set aside while you prepare the pan.

Cube the butter, place it in the pan or pie dish and set in the preheated oven for 8–10 minutes, until the pan's really hot and the butter is sizzling. As soon as the pan is ready, pour in the batter and bake for 20 minutes. When it's ready, the Baby will have majestically puffed and tanned to a golden brown. Serve straight away with the rhubarb (rewarm it if you need to) and plenty of ice cream.

Serves 2

150g rhubarb, cut into 3–4cm chunks

30g caster sugar

½ teaspoon ground cinnamon

1 star anise

For the batter:

50g caster sugar

2 large eggs

100ml milk

60g plain flour

¼ teaspoon ground cinnamon

Pinch of ground nutmeg

Pinch of salt

25g butter

MYSTIC PIZZA

This pizza is at the heart of the film of the same name – one of my favourite coming-of-age movies, in which three teen waitresses working in a small-town pizza joint navigate their difficult last summer together before college. *Mystic Pizza*'s eponymous dish is made to a secret recipe but what we do know is that it's special enough to win a coveted 4-star review from even the most miserly restaurant critic, turning around the pizza parlour's fortunes for good. This version isn't a recreation of the recipe then as much as a homage to it: it's food to feed the soul, to nourish your friends and the friendships you share with them, and to silence even the worst food snobs you know.

First, prepare the dough: mix the flour, yeast and salt together in a large bowl, then pour in the water and oil. Work everything together to form a shaggy dough and leave to rest for 15 minutes.

While the dough rests, heat the oil for the sauce in a small pan over a low heat then add the garlic and oregano. Cook for a couple of minutes before pouring in the passata with a little salt. Leave to simmer, on the lowest heat possible, for at least 15–20 minutes. Don't cut short this cooking time: allowing the sauce to reduce will make it rich and thick enough to hold its own on the pizza. Decant the sauce into a bowl to cool once it has cooked.

Now that the dough has rested, knead it for a solid 10 minutes. Work on an unfloured surface, or the dough will grow dry and tough; push the dough away from you under the heel of your palm, fold it back on itself, turn it and repeat. The specifics don't really matter, but the important thing is that you keep stretching and folding the dough however works best for you, creating a 'net' of gluten that will help the dough to rise and set. After 10 minutes of kneading, the dough ought to be noticeably smoother, softer and more elastic. Place it back in its bowl and cover with cling film. Leave to rise at normal room temperature for around 1½ hours, or until doubled in size.

While the dough rises, prepare the toppings. Heat the oil in a frying pan over a medium heat and fry the beef mince with the chilli and plenty of salt and pepper for 2–3 minutes, until browned all over. Wilt the spinach by pouring boiling water over it in a pan or heatproof bowl, and leaving it to sit for 30 seconds

Makes 2 pizzas

For the dough:
225g strong white flour
1 teaspoon instant dried yeast
½ teaspoon salt
125ml lukewarm water
2 tablespoons olive oil

For the sauce:
1 tablespoon olive oil
1 clove garlic, crushed
1 teaspoon dried oregano
250g passata
Salt, to taste

To top:
1 tablespoon olive oil
175g beef mince
½ teaspoon chilli flakes
100g spinach
2 eggs
100g Cheddar cheese, grated
1 mozzarella ball, torn into chunks
Salt and black pepper, to taste

before draining. Separate the eggs, collecting the two yolks in two separate bowls, and very lightly whisking the whites together in another. Preheat the oven to 240°C/fan 220°C/gas mark 9 and have a couple of large baking trays ready and lightly greased.

Divide the risen dough in half and roll each piece to a large circle roughly 35cm across. You might want to very lightly dust the work surface with flour if the dough sticks, but it should be reasonably easy to roll. Tease the dough out until it stays in shape without springing back. Transfer each of the pizza bases to a prepared baking tray.

Divide the sauce between the pizzas and spread over the top, leaving a small margin around the edges. Sprinkle the Cheddar on next. When you scatter over the beef, mozzarella and spinach, try to leave a small circle uncovered, perhaps 8–9cm across, in the centre of each pizza, arranging the toppings roughly around it (it's into this gap that we'll put the egg a bit later).

Bake the pizzas in the preheated oven for 10–15 minutes, until the crust is golden brown and the toppings are sizzling. Take them out, pour a little of the egg white into the gap you've left in the middle of each and then gently place the yolks right in the centre. You could just break a whole egg onto the pizza, but I find that gives a little too much white, which spreads across the whole thing and even, if you're unlucky, straight off the edge. Bake for a further 2–3 minutes, until the whites are set but the yolks are still runny.

HERBED SALMON AND RICOTTA QUICHE

This light quiche is ideal for a summer picnic, swapping in ricotta in place of the usual cream and matching that brightness with fresh herbs and lemon. The crust is a little crumblier than some thanks to the wholemeal flour, but you'll find it more substantial and full of flavour, too.

Combine the plain and wholemeal flours and the dried herbs in a large bowl. Cube the butter and add it to the flour, rubbing it in with your fingertips until there are no visible pieces of butter remaining. The mixture should be fine and sandy. Add 2 tablespoons of the cold water and cut it into the dry ingredients using a small knife, working everything together until it begins to form small clumps. There should be no dry flour left in the bowl – if there is, add a drop more water.

Wrap the dough in cling film and chill it in the fridge for 20–30 minutes before rolling. Once it's ready, gather the dough into a ball and roll out on a lightly floured work surface to a circle large enough to line the dish or tin. Press the pastry firmly into the base and sides of the tin and trim off any excess. It may be slightly crumbly, but just work slowly, roll carefully and patch up any breaks or holes with more pastry. Prick the base several times with a fork. Place in the fridge for at least 30 minutes to minimise shrinkage during baking. Meanwhile, preheat the oven to 200°C/fan 180°C/gas mark 6.

Once the pastry case is well chilled and the oven is at the right temperature, line the pastry with a sheet of baking parchment and fill with a thick layer of baking weights. Bake for 20 minutes then remove the baking parchment parcel and put the pastry case back in the oven uncovered for a further 5 minutes or so.

While the pastry bakes, wrap the salmon fillets in foil, place on a baking tray and slide onto another oven shelf. Cook for 10–12 minutes – barely long enough for the salmon to start flaking. You don't want to overcook it at this stage.

Wilt the watercress or spinach in a sieve or steamer set over a pan of simmering water. Whisk half of the ricotta together with the double cream, eggs and lemon zest and season generously. Stir in the herbs.

Makes 1 large quiche, serving 8

For the pastry:
100g plain white flour
75g wholemeal flour
2 teaspoons dried parsley or dill
100g salted butter
2–3 tablespoons cold water

For the filling:
2 skinless salmon fillets (roughly 250g)
50g watercress or spinach
250g ricotta
150ml double cream
3 large eggs
Zest of 1 lemon
Couple of small handfuls of fresh parsley, roughly chopped
2–3 dill fronds, roughly chopped
Salt and black pepper, to taste

20–23cm round tart tin, flan dish or spring-form cake tin

Once the pastry and salmon are each cooked, turn the oven down to 180°C/fan 160°C/gas mark 4. Break the salmon into generous chunks and place evenly in the case. Add the wilted greens then dollop the remaining ricotta on top in scattered spoonfuls. Pour over the cream-ricotta mixture and nudge the lot around gently with a spoon to just roughly combine.

Bake the quiche for 35–45 minutes, or until the filling is just barely set in the centre. Leave to cool for at least 30 minutes before eating.

More recipes with eggs:
'Perfect Protein' Roasted Broccoli Quinoa, page 43
Vanilla Rhubarb and Custard Pots, page 116
Roasted Strawberry Cream Pavlovas, page 167
Salted Milk Chocolate Blackberry Mousse Cake, page 169
Brooklyn Cheesecake, page 185
5 Ways with Ice Cream, page 210
Banana Crème Brûlée, page 215
Spiced Rice Pudding, page 219
Korean-inspired Rice Bowls, page 240
Toad in the Hole, page 262
Breakfast Kedgeree, page 271
Coffee Cream Meringue with Cherries, page 345

BUTTER, CREAM AND MILK

ORANGE BLOSSOM PANNA COTTA
WITH STRAWBERRIES

5 WAYS WITH ICE CREAM

BANANA CRÈME BRÛLÉE

EFFORTLESS LEEK LINGUINE
WITH SPICED BUTTER

SPICED RICE PUDDING

This is my comfort food: milkshakes so thick that they stick fast in your straw; whole pints of ice cream studded with chunks of cookie dough; syrupy mochas from chain coffee stores, heaped high with whipped cream; a creamy pasta bake so rich I can barely move after I've scoffed it; custard-drenched cakes and sticky rice pudding. I love the weight of these things, I love the way that they mute even the most strident flavours to a pastel calmness, smoothing over any edges.

I know that there are those who'll decry dairy and all the supposed harm it can do you, but I'd encourage you to tune out those voices. Think with sympathy of the people who preach anti-dairy at you (and who make money from pointing you in the direction of pricier alternatives) next time you eat your Ben & Jerry's in sync with Bridget Jones or sip a mug of cocoa through *The X Factor* on a Saturday night.

ORANGE BLOSSOM PANNA COTTA WITH STRAWBERRIES

The simplicity of panna cotta – it literally translates as 'cooked cream' – isn't something to be messed around with, but a drop or two of orange blossom water (available in most supermarkets) really brings out the delicacy of this dessert. Make sure you leave plenty of cooling and setting time if making these for a special meal.

Cut the gelatine leaves into a few large pieces and soak in cold water for 5 minutes or so, until softened. Meanwhile heat the milk, sugar and orange zest over a low heat until scalding hot.

Drain the liquid from the gelatine pieces then add the gelatine to the hot milk mixture, whisking immediately to combine. Set back over a low heat and bring to the boil. As soon as the mixture starts to simmer, take it off the heat, stir in the single cream and add orange blossom water to taste. Strain the liquid through a fine sieve to remove the orange zest.

Lightly grease the pudding moulds or ramekins and divide the panna cotta mixture between them. Leave to cool to room temperature before placing in the fridge for a few hours to chill and set. I find it's best to leave them overnight, but as long as you can spare 2–3 hours of fridge time, you should be fine.

Once the panna cotta is chilling, quarter the strawberries and toss them in a bowl with the caster sugar and the orange blossom water to taste. Place in the fridge to macerate while the puddings set.

To unmould the panna cotta, carefully dip the bottoms of each basin or ramekin in hot water for a few seconds before inverting the pudding onto a plate. If the panna cotta sticks stubbornly in its mould, try running a small knife around the edge or dipping into the hot water for a few moments more. Serve with the macerated strawberries.

Serves 4

3 leaves gelatine

300ml full-fat milk

90g caster sugar

Coarsely grated zest of
1 orange

100ml single cream

½-1½ teaspoons orange
blossom water, to taste

For the strawberries:

175g strawberries

30g caster sugar

Orange blossom water,
to taste

Four individual 150ml
pudding moulds or ramekins

5 WAYS WITH ICE CREAM

Ice cream is something that I spent a long, long time wanting to make before I finally found the confidence to give it a go. It's a time-consuming thing to do yourself, but my only regret now is having put it off for so long: apart from the waiting while the ice cream freezes, it's deceptively simple to make, and something you can really be proud of once it's done. What's more, you've got total control over what goes into it, so whether you want a subtly flavoured gelato or a more-is-more extravaganza, it's within your reach. You should find it far richer, denser and creamier than even the pricier shop-bought ice creams, too, because it's not whipped up with air.

On the next few pages are five very different recipes, but they all follow the same basic method: make a custard to form the base of the ice cream, chill it and then freeze until set. The make or break step each time is the freezing, when the ice cream's fate – anything from crunchy ice block to soft-scoop – will be decided. The trick is to make sure that the ice cream freezes quickly and evenly, with as few ice crystals as possible. Using a wide, shallow container helps, as does making sure that the ice cream is thoroughly chilled before it enters the freezer. Crucially, if you're not using an ice cream maker (which will continuously churn the custard for you) you'll also need to beat the ice cream really vigorously at regular intervals until it's almost frozen, to break up any crunchy ice crystals.

SMOOTH VANILLA ICE CREAM

This simple vanilla ice cream forms the base of each of the variations that follow. It's a good starter recipe if you're new to the ice cream making process. Although it's a plain ice cream, you can – and indeed, should – gussy it up with cones, sprinkles, syrups and sauces, wafer biscuits, cookie sandwiches, flakes and decorations to your heart's content.

First, make the custard for the ice cream base. Heat the milk over a low heat until scalding hot, but not boiling. Meanwhile, whisk the egg yolks, caster sugar and cornflour together in a large bowl. Once the milk's hot and the egg yolks are smoothly mixed, slowly pour the milk into the egg yolks, whisking continuously. Decant the custard back into the pan and cook over a very low heat, stirring non-stop, until it's slightly thickened and creamy. Pour into a clean bowl, stir in the vanilla extract and leave to cool to room temperature.

Once the custard is cool, move it to the fridge to chill for at least an hour. When it's well chilled, stir in the double cream.

You can freeze your ice cream, either in an ice cream maker following the manufacturer's instructions or by hand in the freezer. If churning by hand, first tip the custard into a wide tub (the shallower the layer of ice cream, the quicker it'll freeze) then move it to the freezer. Freeze for 30 minutes, then beat generously using a fork to break up any ice crystals. Repeat this freezing and churning at 30–45-minute intervals, until the ice cream is very thick and almost frozen. This shouldn't take any longer than 2–3 hours. Now you can leave the ice cream to freeze completely. Take the ice cream from the freezer 10–15 minutes before you serve to give it a chance to soften a little.

Makes 750ml, enough for six servings

400ml full-fat milk

4 egg yolks

150g caster sugar

1 tablespoon cornflour

1 tablespoon vanilla extract

300ml double cream

GINGER BISCUIT CRUNCH

Some ginger biscuits are crushed and added straight to the custard base here, while the rest are added in chunks once the ice cream has almost frozen – it's the best way to blend in the spiced, caramel flavour whilst keeping a textural contrast. Just make the custard as on page 211, replacing the 150g caster sugar with 125g soft light brown sugar, and throwing in a tablespoon of ground ginger. Crush 100g ginger biscuits to a powder and stir into the mixture while it's still warm. Leave to cool and chill, then add the double cream as above. Freeze and churn the custard, adding another 100g ginger biscuits – this time broken into small chunks – when the ice cream is nearly completely frozen.

CINNAMON AND BURNT HONEY

First, simmer 100g good-quality runny honey over a low heat for 3–5 minutes, until it's fragrant and has darkened a shade. As soon as it's ready, whisk in 300ml double cream, then leave to cool. Make the custard as in the vanilla version on page 211, but replace the 150g caster sugar with just 40g soft light brown sugar and add 1 teaspoon of ground cinnamon along with the cornflour. Let the custard cool and chill, then stir in the honey and cream mixture once it's cold. Freeze as in the vanilla version.

INTENSE CHOCOLATE AND CARDAMOM

To the standard vanilla custard on page 211, add 4 tablespoons of cocoa powder and the finely crushed seeds from 8 cardamom pods along with the cornflour. Very finely chop 100g dark chocolate and heat the double cream until scalding; pour the cream over the chopped chocolate and stir until melted and smooth. Mix the chocolate and cream mixture into the custard while both are still warm, then leave to cool to room temperature, chill, and freeze as in the vanilla version.

BLUEBERRY CHEESECAKE SWIRL

You'll never again have to break your heart choosing between cheesecake and ice cream for dessert. Make the basic custard as on page 211, but use an extra 75g caster sugar and another tablespoon of cornflour. Chill the custard in the fridge. In place of the 300ml double cream, beat together 300g cream cheese (it just has to be full-fat) with 150ml sour cream and 150ml double cream, then stir through the chilled custard until smooth. Freeze as in the vanilla version.

While the ice cream freezes, combine 150g blueberries and 2 tablespoons caster sugar in a small pan with a splash of water and cook gently until the blueberries are bursting. Whisk 2 teaspoons of cornflour with 2 teaspoons of water in a separate bowl, then stir this into the blueberry mixture. Cook for a further minute to thicken the juices. Remove from the heat and leave to cool. This will be the blueberry compote to swirl through the ice cream later.

For a biscuit rubble to ripple the ice cream like a cheesecake's biscuit base, finely crush 100g digestive biscuits and stir together with 60g melted butter. Press firmly onto a parchment-lined baking tray in a layer a little less than 1cm thick and bake at 180°C/fan 160°C/gas mark 4 for 10 minutes. Leave to cool.

Stir the blueberry compote very gently through the ice cream when it's nearly frozen, and crumble the biscuit base through in crumbs and chunks. Work slowly and don't overmix, or the swirls will lose their definition and bleed into the ice cream. Leave to freeze completely, softening for 10 minutes before serving. This will make 8–10 servings rather than the six specified in the vanilla version.

BANANA CRÈME BRÛLÉE

This dessert is glorified bananas-and-custard, really, but I don't see that as any bad thing. If you want to refine this for a more grown-up palate, try adding a little ground cardamom, or even replace the vanilla extract with vanilla pods, split and added to the heating cream to infuse (I know it's just appearances but I always feel it's far fancier if I can see that delicate freckling of tiny vanilla seeds through the custard).

Preheat the oven to 150°C/fan 130°C/gas mark 2. Warm the cream over a low heat until scalding hot but not boiling. In a mixing bowl, mash half of the bananas – you'll need roughly 125g – then whisk with the egg yolks, half the sugar and the vanilla extract.

Pour the hot cream into the banana and egg mixture, whisking all the while, then strain through a fine sieve to catch any rogue lumps. Cut the remaining banana into slices no greater than 1cm thick and divide between the ramekins. Pour the custard over the top, and don't worry if the ramekins aren't full to the brim.

Place the filled ramekins in a small baking dish or roasting tin and pour just enough hot water into the dish to reach two-thirds of the way up the outside of the ramekins. This water will act as a shield against the heat of the oven, ensuring that the custards cook evenly. Cook the custards in the oven until well set – there should be no more than the slightest of wobbles at their centres. This should take 30–35 minutes, but it pays to keep a close eye on them in case your oven runs hot or cold.

Carefully take the custards out of the water bath and leave to cool to room temperature before transferring to the fridge to chill. Once chilled, dredge the remaining caster sugar over the top and either grill or blowtorch them until the sugar has melted, bubbled and browned. You'll have most control over the rate and degree of caramelisation if you use a mini blowtorch, but the grill will do a fine job too as long as you preheat it thoroughly so that it's searing hot when you place the custards under it.

Once the tops have caramelised to a mottled sugar crust, chill the custards for a short while then serve.

Makes 4

300ml double cream

2 medium/large bananas, peeled

4 large egg yolks

75g caster sugar

2 teaspoons vanilla extract

Four ovenproof ramekins

EFFORTLESS LEEK LINGUINE WITH SPICED BUTTER

The amount of butter in this dish isn't gratuitous, though I'd be lying if I said it doesn't give me a thrill to scoop spoonfuls into the hot pan and watch it sink into molten gold. Leeks need a lot of butter (and it really does have to be butter, not oil) as they fry to help them gently soften and collapse into a silky mess. If you scrimp on the fat and let the leek brown and burn, it'll quickly become so bitter that the whole dish will be inedible. Be patient, cautious with the heat and generous with the butter.

Melt the butter in a large, heavy-based pan over a low heat. Add the spices, whisk to combine then throw in the leeks. Keeping the heat very low, place a lid on the pan and leave to cook for 15 minutes, or until the leeks are silky and soft, stirring occasionally.

Cook the pasta in a pan of boiling salted water and drain, retaining a couple of tablespoons of the cooking water. Add the linguine and reserved pasta water to the leeks, then stir in the crème fraîche and a couple of tablespoons of shaved Parmesan. Serve straight away with extra Parmesan.

Serves 4

100g butter

1 teaspoon sweet paprika

½ teaspoon grated nutmeg

Pinch of chilli powder

3 leeks, trimmed and thickly sliced

400g linguine

4 tablespoons crème fraîche

Plenty of shaved Parmesan

SPICED RICE PUDDING

The advantage of this stove-top rice pudding over the usual oven-baked types is that although it needs more hands-on attention, it cooks more quickly and more creamily than you might be used to. This spiced version uses cardamom and cinnamon to lend warmth to the pudding's milky sweetness and, unusually, calls for the addition of egg yolks at the end of the cooking time, leaving it velvety smooth, golden and rich.

Combine the rice and water in a spacious, heavy-based pan and set over a medium heat. Cook, stirring occasionally, until most of the water has been absorbed; this shouldn't take longer than 10 minutes or so. Next, add the milk and spices and bring to the boil. Once the liquid reaches a simmer, reduce the heat slightly and cook slowly for 25 minutes, until the rice is tender but not mushy. Remember to stir every few minutes, or the milk will catch on the base of the pan.

Once the pudding's thickened, add the sugar followed by the egg yolks, whisking continuously as you add the egg so that it doesn't scramble on contact with the hot milk. Serve hot or cold, slackening with a little more milk if it sets too solid.

Serves 4 generously

150g short grain or pudding rice

250ml water

850ml full-fat milk

4 cardamom pods, lightly crushed

1 cinnamon stick

100g caster sugar

3 egg yolks, lightly beaten

More recipes with butter, cream and milk:

MEAT
AND FISH

CHICKEN

5 WAYS WITH CHICKEN WINGS

SELF-CARE CHICKEN SOUP

GHANAIAN GROUNDNUT CHICKEN STEW

STICKY CHILLI AND PEANUT
FRIED CHICKEN

ROAST CHICKEN WITH FENNEL,
LEMON AND CREAM

I've started this chapter with chicken because it feels like a good entry point into carnivorous cooking. Until relatively recently, I'd hardly cooked with meat: between a largely vegetarian upbringing, a brief spell of veganism and a tight food budget as a student, meat barely figured in my diet or my kitchen, and the foods I felt most confident with were hearty vegetarian dishes. When I finished university, though, and pushed myself to try new things, I decided to branch out and learn how to cook well with meat and poultry. Because it has a less overwhelming flavour and is easy to cook, chicken was my first baby step into this new culinary territory. I quickly became comfortable deep-frying batches of drumsticks, roasting the whole bird with veg and herbs, and simmering handfuls of wings into flavourful stocks, as well as marinating, frying, grilling, poaching and stir-frying it in as many ways as I could think of. If you're not a seasoned meat cook, start here.

Though it's milder than other poultry – not too gamey, salty or dark – it would be wrong to mistake chicken for a blank canvas. The lighter breast meat is more delicate than the brown leg meat, but both have a delicious flavour of their own. This ought to be clear from the way that even the most lazily roasted chicken can hold its own against the myriad vegetables, gravy, potatoes and stuffing heaped alongside it. The trick is in how you cook it, though, because no amount of good flavour will redeem a chalky, overcooked chicken. It helps to buy a chicken that's been well raised and well fed, too, for the plumpest birds with the tastiest meat. You needn't spend a fortune on a top-quality chicken every single time you cook (if you're deep-frying it or partnering the meat with a salty, spicy marinade, rub or sauce, any flavour nuance from a more expensive bird will likely be lost), but just be mindful of the provenance of the meat you use, and look out for higher-welfare chicken where you can.

5 WAYS WITH CHICKEN WINGS

It's a really specific formula that makes chicken wings so popular and so moreish. Apart from livers, they're the cheapest supermarket-available part of the chicken, which is a huge pro when it comes to feeding many mouths and feeding them well. Though wings can be a little fiddly, their bite-sized proportions make them perfect for informal finger food feasts, and give them a greater surface area for taking on the flavour of tasty spicy rubs, marinades and glazes. What's more, the meat, though scant, is flavourful and sweet and because there's such a high skin-to-meat ratio, the wings are richer, fattier and more tender than other cuts of the bird. They're not for the squeamish or those who don't like getting their hands dirty, but if you don't mind the mess and the hands-on eating, these could be your new favourite midweek dinner.

SIMPLE CRISP SPICED CHICKEN WINGS

This simple recipe encrusts the wings with a smoky spice blend for an easy flavour fix. Adjust the amounts of the spices however you please to strike a perfect balance between smokiness, sweetness and heat, but don't leave out the flour – this helps to draw moisture out, giving a crisp skin. Use the basic method below to guide you through the four other chicken wing recipes over the coming pages.

Preheat the oven to 200°C/fan 180°C/gas mark 6 and line a baking tray with foil.

Using a pair of large scissors or a sharp knife, clip the wing tips from the chicken: these are the spindly final sections at the end of the wing, though if you've sourced yours straight from the butcher they may already have been trimmed.

Stir together the flour, paprika, cayenne, celery salt and white pepper for the spice blend. Toss the chicken wings in the melted butter to coat, then sprinkle the spice mix all over the wings, top and bottom. Rub the spice into the skin.

Bake the wings for 45 minutes, turning them halfway through the cooking time.

Serves 3–4

12 chicken wings

1 tablespoon plain flour

1 teaspoon smoked paprika

1 teaspoon cayenne pepper

½ teaspoon celery salt

½ teaspoon ground white pepper

50g butter, melted

MISO CHILLI CHICKEN WINGS

Miso is a Japanese fermented soy bean paste, which gives
a wonderful savoury hit to this wing recipe, especially when
partnered with the sweetness of mirin (Japanese rice wine) and
honey. These might seem like unusual ingredients, but I promise
that they're easy to get hold of: where I live in Essex, I find them
in the 'World Foods' section of my local supermarket. Make the
marinade by combining 5 tablespoons of mirin, 4 tablespoons
of miso paste, 3 tablespoons of runny honey and ½ teaspoon
of chilli flakes. Sit the trimmed chicken wings in the marinade
for at least 2 hours in the fridge. Bake for 45 minutes at
200°C/fan 180°C/gas mark 6, turning and basting with a
little leftover marinade halfway through.

STICKY BBQ WINGS

For 12 wings, trimmed as in the recipe opposite, whisk together
a marinade of 4 tablespoons of ketchup, 4 tablespoons of
Worcestershire sauce, 2 tablespoons of maple syrup, 1 tablespoon
of Dijon mustard and 2 crushed cloves of garlic. Mix the wings
with the marinade in a plastic tub or large freezer bag and leave to
marinate for at least 2 hours and up to 12 hours in the fridge. Bake
as in the main recipe opposite, but pour over any excess marinade
just after you've turned them, halfway through the cooking time.

SOY AND GINGER SESAME WINGS

Clip the wing tips from 12 wings then marinate in 4 tablespoons of light soy sauce, 8–9cm fresh ginger (peeled and grated), 5 tablespoons of runny honey and 4 crushed cloves of garlic for 2–12 hours in the fridge. Bake for 45 minutes, as on page 224. When half the cooking time has elapsed turn the wings, baste them with any leftover marinade and sprinkle over a couple of tablespoons of sesame seeds. Serve with plenty of finely sliced spring onion.

GARLICKY LEMON AND HERB WINGS

This is a little brighter and more summery in flavour than the recipes above, with aniseed-y tarragon, dill, and plenty of fresh parsley and lemon giving life to the marinade. Mix the juice and zest of 2 lemons, a tablespoon of Dijon mustard, 2 crushed cloves of garlic and plenty of salt and coarsely ground black pepper. Finely chop the leaves from 4 fronds of dill, 4 sprigs of tarragon and a handful of parsley and stir into the marinade. Trim the chicken wings as detailed on page 224, then marinate in the lemon and herb mixture in the fridge for at least 2 hours. Bake for 45 minutes in a 200°C/fan 180°C/gas mark 6 oven, turning the wings over after 20–25 minutes.

SELF-CARE CHICKEN SOUP

In *Heartburn*, Meryl Streep's character makes Jack Nicholson's character a huge plate of spaghetti carbonara in the early hours of the morning after their first night together. She pads into the bedroom and sets it down in front of him on the bed, and he starts talking about how they're going to be married. In *Moonstruck*, Cher takes control in a young Nicholas Cage's kitchen, raiding his fridge to make him a steak, whether he likes it or not. Apart from the outfit inspiration, the one take-home message from ultimate teen movie *Clueless* is that you should always have something baking in the oven when a date comes round.

I love this theme of nurturing through food. There's something so special about manifesting your love for someone in the form of food: nourishing them and giving them strength through something you've crafted with your own hands. We need to remember to set aside some of that energy for ourselves too, though, putting self-care back on to the menu rather than always putting the needs of others first. Here's a chicken soup with incredible restorative powers – not just in terms of nutrition but in the cathartic slowness of actually making it – that I cook for myself when I most need strength, love and care.

There's something about the heft of this soup – lowering a whole chicken into a stockpot – that makes this recipe seem much more hassle than it really is. The truth is that as soon as you've got the ingredients in the pot, the hard work is over.

You can eat this either as a clear broth or as a more substantial soup. If you want some vegetable chunks, I'd recommend chopping and adding them after the broth has been cooked and the herbs, old veg and chicken carcass removed: vegetables that have cooked for 2½ hours with the chicken will be very mushy and grey, so it's best to cook some fresh in the broth, just simmering for 10–15 minutes until tender. Other possible additions include matzo ball dumplings (you can find packet mixes for these in the supermarket) and soup pasta such as macaroni or broken spaghetti shards.

Serves 4

1 small chicken

2 onions, halved

2 celery sticks, cut into large chunks

2 large carrots, cut into large chunks

4 bay leaves

Small bunch of parsley

Small bunch of dill

Salt and black pepper

Throw all of the ingredients into a large stockpot and add enough
water to cover. Set over a medium heat and, once the stock
reaches a simmer, turn the heat down to low so the liquid is
barely simmering, loosely cover with a lid and leave to cook gently
for 2½ hours.

Carefully pluck the chicken from the broth and set it on a baking
dish to rest. Strain the broth through a fine sieve, collecting all of
the liquid and leaving behind the herbs and veg. Season the broth
generously and set over a very low heat while you carefully skin
the chicken and pluck the meat from the bone. Reheat some
of the chicken in the broth before serving.

GHANAIAN GROUNDNUT CHICKEN STEW

In this West African stew, chicken is cooked in a thick peanut (or groundnut) sauce, brought to life with fiery scotch bonnet pepper and hot ginger. I make this with my Ghanaian grandad in mind, though because I've never actually been to the motherland myself I can't promise that this is a completely authentic version. And yet I'm not sure that authenticity is really the point here: it's just about connecting with your heritage, wherever that lies, and eating to feed your soul.

Heat the oil in a large pan and fry the chicken pieces over a medium-high heat for 8–10 minutes, turning halfway, until they are golden brown on each side. If you crowd the chicken, it'll steam instead of browning, so cook in batches if your pan isn't big enough.

Set the browned meat aside and fry the onions and peppers in the same pan over a low-medium heat, adding a splash more oil if you need to. After 10 minutes, add the garlic and ginger. Pierce the scotch bonnet pepper a few times to help it release a little of that blast of heat, then add it, whole, to the pan. Cook for a couple more minutes before adding the peanut butter and tomato purée. Once everything is well combined, slowly pour in the chicken stock and return the chicken pieces to the pan. Add a little extra hot water if the liquid doesn't quite cover the meat.

Put a lid on the pan, turn down the heat and leave to simmer for 25–30 minutes, stirring often. Taste the sauce as you go to check the level of spice, and take out the scotch bonnet if the heat gets too much. Remove the lid and reduce for 5 minutes before serving with plenty of rice and a topping of salted peanuts and fresh coriander.

Serves 4

2 tablespoons olive oil

8 chicken thighs or drumsticks, skinless

2 medium onions, finely chopped

2 red peppers, diced

4 cloves garlic, crushed

6cm fresh ginger, grated

1 scotch bonnet chilli pepper

150g smooth peanut butter

6 tablespoons tomato purée

600ml chicken stock

50g roasted salted peanuts

Small handful of coriander leaves, roughly chopped

STICKY CHILLI AND PEANUT FRIED CHICKEN

Chicken has had its name dragged through the dirt by recipes that celebrate it only for its low-fat credentials (think sorry-looking skinless chicken breast fillets grilled to greyness, stringy with despair, served with salad leaves). I'm here to sort that out, by deep-frying it, tossing it in a sweet-salty chilli sauce and scattering the sticky chicken morsels with roasted peanuts. Deep-frying can be intimidating, but check the guide on page 94 if you're worried.

I use *gochujang*, which is a Korean fermented rice and chilli paste, to give a kick to the sauce. It gives a good balance of heat and savouriness, unlike some other chilli sauces which can err on sickly sweetness. You can use whatever chilli condiment you have to hand, though, just make sure that you adjust the amount you use depending on how hot it is. You may also want a little less ketchup or sugar, or a splash more soy sauce, to fine tune the sauce as you go.

Let the chicken stand at room temperature for half an hour (this will help it to cook evenly upon contact with the hot oil). While the chicken rests, pour the oil into a large, heavy-based pan (preferably not a non-stick one) or deep fryer and heat until it reaches 180°C, using a kitchen thermometer to monitor the oil's temperature if you're heating it on the hob.

Combine 100g of the plain flour with the cornflour, garlic, cayenne, black pepper and salt in a wide bowl. Drizzle in the soy sauce and work in with your fingers to leave the flour very slightly clumpy. Beat the egg with the milk in a separate bowl. Roll the chicken pieces first in the remaining 75g plain flour, then in the egg mixture, then in the spiced and seasoned flour mixture until well coated all over. Don't be scared to get a good, thick coat on the chicken, and leave on any clumps because these will crisp up really well for a crunchy texture when they fry.

When the oil is at the right temperature, carefully lower a few drumsticks in and fry in batches for 12–14 minutes, until the juices at the thickest part of the meat run clear when pierced with a small knife. Leave to cool for 30 minutes (or they can be

Serves 4–6

12 chicken drumsticks

2 litres vegetable or corn oil

175g plain flour

50g cornflour

3 cloves garlic, crushed

1 teaspoon cayenne pepper

½ teaspoon ground black pepper

½ teaspoon salt

4 teaspoons light soy sauce

1 large egg

2 tablespoons milk

For the sauce:

200g tomato ketchup

100g soft dark brown sugar

80ml light soy sauce

1 tablespoon wholegrain mustard

1–4 tablespoons hot chilli sauce, depending on the heat of the brand you use

2 teaspoons white wine vinegar

3 cloves garlic, crushed

60g roasted salted peanuts

kept in the fridge for up to 24 hours, if you're preparing these in advance), then fry again at 180°C for 10 minutes just before you're ready to eat them. The first fry cooks the chicken, the second crisps the outside; if you were to cook the drumsticks for one long, continuous spell in the hot oil, the meat would overcook before the outside had had a chance to get crunchy.

While the chicken fries for a second time, combine all of the ingredients for the sauce in a small pan and set over a low heat until bubbling. Once the drumsticks are ready, pour the sauce all over them and toss to coat, then scatter the peanuts over to finish.

ROAST CHICKEN WITH FENNEL, LEMON AND CREAM

Because it's cooked with the fennel in cream and stock, the chicken in this one-dish dinner stays perfectly tender and moist. It's an easy way to cook meat, veg and sauce all in one, sidestepping the effort of a traditional roast chicken while keeping all of the flavour. Give this a go even if you're not typically keen on fennel: the cream and Parmesan mellow the aniseed flavour, while the process of roasting brings fennel's sweeter edge to the fore.

Preheat the oven to 200°C/fan 180°C/gas mark 6. Trim the leafy tops off the fennel, remove any tough outer layers and slice each bulb in 1cm-thick wedges. Arrange the fennel wedges and chicken drumsticks in the oven dish and scatter over the sliced basil.

Stir together the double cream, stock, 75g of the Parmesan and the lemon zest, then season with salt and pepper to taste. Pour this creamy stock over the top of the chicken and bake for 45 minutes, turning the drumsticks halfway through. Ten minutes before the end of the cooking time, sprinkle over the remaining Parmesan before returning to the oven to brown. Serve with mash or steamed new potatoes and greens.

Serves 4

4 fennel bulbs

8 skinless chicken drumsticks

Leaves from a small bunch of basil, finely sliced

225ml double cream

450ml chicken stock

100g grated Parmesan

Zest of 1 lemon

Salt and black pepper, to taste

20x30cm oven dish or roasting tin

More recipes with chicken:
One-pot Red Peppers with Chicken, page 37
Zesty Lime Chicken with Peach Salsa, page 153

BEEF

KOREAN-INSPIRED RICE BOWLS

5 WAYS WITH BEEFBURGERS

STEAMED BEEF AND ALE PUDDING

BRIGHT BEEF NOODLE SALAD
WITH CHILLI LIME DRESSING

ADÈLE'S SPAGHETTI BOLOGNESE

BEEF RENDANG

It's not my style to cook or eat big cuts of meat: I don't much like steak or chops; I'd rather eat a casserole, curry or stew than a rack of ribs or a roast any day. The recipes in this section are my attempt at reconciling these tastes, making beef more manageable in chunks, morsels and mince, while keeping all of that deeply savoury heft that makes it so delicious. Because it's such a powerful flavour, beef can stand up to some punchy ingredients. In this section, I've paired it with coconut and chilli, ale, lime, anchovy and harissa. With each of these very different flavours, you'll experience a different side of beef: sometimes dark and caramelised, sometimes deeply savoury, sometimes iron-rich and tangy.

KOREAN-INSPIRED RICE BOWLS

I've clumsily called these 'Korean-inspired' because, while they're based on *bibimbap* (Korean rice and veg bowls), I wanted to establish a distance between my Anglicised version of the dish and the real deal. Made with whatever ingredients I can get hold of in the supermarket, this recipe is a long way from a genuine bibimbap but is a beautiful way of serving rice nonetheless – topped with garlicky vegetables and chilli beef, drizzled with spicy *gochujang* (see page 235 for more information and alternatives) and finished with a sunny fried egg. There are several components to this dish, but each one is simple and there's no great amount of multitasking or juggling necessary: keep the elements warm in a low oven while you get everything ready, then heap the rainbow of veg and meat onto the rice when you're ready to eat. You can swap in different meat and vegetables if you want – perhaps aubergine sliced into thin rounds and fried with garlic, slivers of sliced, stir-fried pak choi, or a fistful of sprouted seeds – but make sure that you keep the colours and textures varied: this dish is a game of contrasts, and it's these surprises that make it special.

First, make the rice: rinse it several times under cold running water, then place in a large, heavy-based pan with 550ml water. Set over a medium-high heat and bring to a simmer. As soon as the water reaches the boil, turn the heat down to low and put a lid on the pan. Cook for a further 10 minutes, then turn off the heat and – leaving the lid firmly on the pan – let the rice sit and steam for 30 minutes. It's crucial that you don't take off the lid and let the steam escape while the rice cooks or rests.

While the rice is steaming, prepare the meat and vegetables. Turn the oven on to a very low heat to keep the prepared components warm while you work. Heat a little sesame oil in a pan and fry the beef mince with the chilli and 1 of the crushed cloves of garlic over a medium-high heat until the mince is well browned. Decant into a clean bowl and place in the oven to keep warm.

Fry the carrot in a good glug of sesame oil with the other clove of crushed garlic for 3 minutes then season and set aside. In a bowl, toss the courgette slices with salt, leave to sit for 10 minutes to draw out the water, then fry for a couple of minutes with a little sesame oil. Pour boiling water over the spinach to wilt it, then

Serves 4

400g sushi rice

Sesame oil, for frying

250g beef mince

½ red chilli, deseeded and finely chopped

2 cloves garlic, crushed

1 carrot, cut into matchsticks

1 courgette, cut into long, thin slices

¼ teaspoon salt

150g spinach

150g beansprouts

4 eggs

4 radishes, thinly sliced

Salt, to taste

To dress:

4 tablespoons gochujang or other mild chilli paste/sauce

2 tablespoons caster sugar

1½ tablespoons sesame oil

drain and season generously with salt and sesame oil. Fry the beansprouts over a high heat with a drop of sesame oil for 1–2 minutes. Keep all these components warm in the low oven once they're ready.

For the dressing, whisk together the gochujang (or whatever chilli sauce you're using), sugar and sesame oil.

Place a mound of rice into the middle of four largish bowls. Fry the eggs until the white is set but the yolk runny, and while they cook, arrange the prepared beef, carrot, courgette, spinach, beansprouts and radish slices in distinct piles on top of the rice. Set the fried eggs, sunny side up, on top of the lot and drizzle the sauce over each bowl. Serve straight away.

5 WAYS WITH BEEFBURGERS

There's a moment in the music video for 'Feeling Myself' when Beyoncé and Nicki Minaj crook their arms through each other's and, hooked close together, simultaneously bite into two burgers. Watch it and you'll never again see burgers as trash, junk food or a cop-out meal, but an ambrosial feast.

If you're hankering for a burger right now – if you can almost taste the salt on your tongue and feel the grease on your fingers – it's already too late for this recipe. I totally support your adventures in homemade food, but it's so important to satisfy your cravings as they hit: if you need a burger asap, go to McDonald's, go to Burger King, go to the chip shop, go wherever, and get it. If you're in the mood for a little project, though, these easy beefburger recipes are fun, quick and delicious.

ORIGINAL BEEFBURGERS

Because there are only three ingredients in these basic burger patties, it's worth using good-quality beef mince if you can afford it. That said, food snobbery has no place between the halves of a bun so if all you've got to hand is the cheap stuff, just go for it. As long as you show your burger the care it deserves – an attentive spell in the frying pan, thoughtful seasoning, loaded with all the trimmings – it'll be a feast no matter your budget.

In a large bowl, mix the beef, onion and salt gently but thoroughly using your hands. Preheat a drop of oil in a large heavy-based frying pan over a medium heat. Fry a small chunk of the burger mix in the hot oil to check the seasoning, and add extra salt or a dose of black pepper as you see fit. Shape the burger mix into 12 patties, each 2–3cm thick.

Heat a bit of oil in the pan and fry each burger patty for 4–5 minutes on each side, adjusting the heat as necessary to get a burger that's well browned on the outside but juicy within. If you're making cheeseburgers, slap a slice of Cheddar on top of the patty once it's been flipped, halfway through cooking.

Makes 12 burger patties

1kg beef mince

1 large onion, coarsely grated

½ teaspoon salt

Black pepper, to taste (optional)

Vegetable oil, for frying

CARROT AND HERB BURGERS

If you're looking to smuggle a little goodness into a fussy eater's burgers, try adding 300g finely grated carrot (from 3–4 medium carrots) and 3 tablespoons of finely chopped parsley to the mix. Cook as on page 243.

HOT HARISSA BURGERS

For a sweet-hot zing, add 4 tablespoons of harissa paste and two deseeded, finely chopped red chillies to the beef and forget about the onion. These burgers work well in pitta breads, if you don't fancy a traditional burger bun.

CHILLI-SPICED FENNEL SEED BURGERS

In spite of the trio of big flavours inside them, these garlic-laced burgers are a more delicate alternative to the usual savoury oniony variety. Just leave out the grated onion and swap in three teaspoons of fennel seeds, finely ground, three small cloves of crushed garlic and ½ teaspoon of hot chilli powder, or more or less to taste.

CHORIZO BURGERS

This one's easy – just throw in 200g finely chopped chorizo and 2 teaspoons of smoked paprika to the beef. A dash of cayenne pepper wouldn't go amiss, either.

STEAMED BEEF AND ALE PUDDING

Making a steamed pudding is a labour of love, but if you can muster the energy you'll find the process – rolling pastry, swaddling the basin in baking parchment and rough twine and watching closely as it simmers and steams – every bit as comforting as the end result. This is food to warm, to cheer and to comfort.

Heat the oil in a large pan, add the onion and carrot with a pinch of salt and cook over a medium-low heat for 15–20 minutes, until the onions are soft.

While the vegetables cook, toss the beef with the flour to coat then fry in a large pan over a high heat for barely a minute or two – just long enough to begin to brown the edges of the meat. The meat needn't be browned all over; in fact, if you wait that long you risk overcooking and toughening it. It's best to fry in batches to avoid crowding the meat in the pan, and remember to stir continuously.

Transfer the browned meat to the pan with the onion and carrot, off the heat. Add a little of the beef stock and stout to the pan in which you fried the meat and let it bubble for a couple of minutes while you scrape off any browned bits from the bottom of the pan (all of this will give the pudding more flavour). Add this mixture to the beef and onions along with the remaining stock and stout, the Marmite and the rosemary needles.

Set the pan over a low heat and cover loosely with a lid. Simmer for 2 hours, never letting the mixture bubble too fiercely. As the mixture enters its last half hour of cooking, add the diced potato. When the meat is tender, turn off the heat and leave to cool.

For the pastry, combine the flour, baking powder, salt and suet in a large bowl and add enough of the water to bring the mixture to a firm but pliable dough. Use your hands to combine, as this gives you a better sense of the consistency. Take care not to knead the pastry, though, or it risks becoming tough.

Grease the pudding basin and line the base with a circle of baking parchment, to prevent the pudding sticking at the bottom. Roll out three-quarters of the pastry until no more than 5mm thick and drape it into the pudding basin, trimming off any excess and

Serves 4

3 tablespoons vegetable oil

1 large onion, thinly sliced

1 large carrot, cut into chunks

400g braising steak, cut into largish chunks

2 tablespoons plain flour

200ml beef stock

150ml stout

1 teaspoon Marmite

Leaves from 1 sprig of rosemary

1 medium potato, peeled and diced

Salt, to taste

For the suet pastry:

300g plain flour

3 teaspoons baking powder

½ teaspoon salt

150g suet

150–175ml water

0.75–1 litre pudding basin

pressing the pastry neatly into the sides. Fill with the cooled beef mixture, taking care to leave room at the top so that the pudding doesn't bubble over. Roll the remaining portion of pastry to a circle large enough to cover the top. Brush a little water around the rim of the pastry then press into place, pinching the pastry sides and lid together to seal. Cover the pudding with a sheet of baking parchment, with a wide pleat folded down the middle to allow room for the pudding to rise. Secure in place with a length of string tied around the basin. Repeat with a layer of foil.

Place a small jam jar lid or metal pastry cutter in the base of a large pan, add 10cm or so of water and set over a medium heat. Once the water has reached a steady boil, place the pudding basin on top of the jar lid or pastry cutter (this keeps the basin away from the direct heat at the base of the pan). Add more water (or take a little out, if necessary) so that it reaches halfway up the sides of the pudding basin. Place a lid on the pan and steam the pudding for 2 hours.

When it's ready, remove the pudding basin from the pan and gently tease off the foil and baking parchment. Very gently loosen the tops of the sides with a small knife. Place a large plate upside down on top of the pudding and in one swift motion (easier than it sounds) invert the pudding onto the plate. When you pull off the pudding basin – this should be easy if it was lined and well greased – you should be faced with a proud, golden brown pudding. Serve immediately with peas or greens.

BRIGHT BEEF NOODLE SALAD WITH CHILLI LIME DRESSING

This recipe is based on Vietnamese noodle salads, playing savoury, sweet and sour against one another in every mouthful: first there's punchy lime juice, then the savoury clout of fish sauce, peanuts and seared beef, next chilli heat and finally the freshness of coriander, basil and mint. It's deceptively filling for a salad, and a good way of making a little meat go a long way.

I've been deliberately vague about the kind of steak to use here, because I don't want this recipe to get tangled in paranoia about 'good' and 'bad' meat, and I don't think there's any point shelling out for the most expensive steak if it's going to be cut into strips and tossed through a salad. Just use whatever frying steak (not the tougher casserole or braising steak) you can afford and cook it for as short a time as you can, depending on how rare, or otherwise, you like it.

I quite like the cleansing heat of the chillies, but if you don't want too much spice, just deseed them.

Gather together and prepare the vegetables and herbs. Fry the steaks in a drop of oil for 2–2½ minutes on each side over a medium heat, or until they are cooked with just a little pink in the middle (of course, cook them more or less according to your tastes, but bear in mind that you'll have to slice them into strips after cooking, which is more difficult with a rare steak). Set the steaks aside to rest for 5 minutes while you prepare the noodles.

Place the noodles into a heatproof dish or bowl, pour boiling water over them and leave for 3 minutes to rehydrate. Drain and rinse under cold water to cool. Slice the rested steak into ½–1cm-wide slivers.

For the dressing, whisk together the fish sauce, lime juice and sugar, then crush in the garlic with the chilli (you can very finely chop the garlic and chilli if you don't have a garlic crusher). Heap the prepared red onion, carrots, chilli, coriander, basil and mint on top of the noodles in a serving dish. Scatter over the beef, spring onions and peanuts, then pour the dressing over the lot. Toss gently together before serving.

Serves 4

½ red onion, thinly sliced

2 carrots, cut into matchsticks

1 red chilli, thinly sliced into rounds

2 handfuls of coriander leaves

Handful of basil leaves

Handful of mint leaves

2 medium beef frying steaks, roughly 400g in total

Vegetable oil, to grease the pan

125g flat rice noodles

2 spring onions, cut into long, thin strips

60g roasted salted peanuts

For the dressing:

4 tablespoons fish sauce

Juice of 2 limes

3 tablespoons caster sugar

2 cloves garlic

1 red chilli

ADÈLE'S SPAGHETTI BOLOGNESE

Everyone should have an inspirational eater to look up to: someone to remind you how much joy there is in eating exactly what you want as greedily, messily and shamelessly as you please. My favourite is Adèle in *Blue is the Warmest Colour*. Whether at home or in public, alone or with a date, she eats with totally unembarrassed hunger. One dish that pops up throughout the film is spaghetti bolognese, which Adèle eats sloppily, asking for seconds, licking the scraps from her knife and barely pausing to wipe sauce off her chin. Be an inspirational eater yourself with this bolognese.

The anchovy fillets in this meaty sauce aren't traditional, but you needn't worry that they'll overpower the dish. They're barely detectable in the finished ragù, just adding a welcome savouriness to complement the beef and to balance the acidic sweetness of the tomato.

Heat the butter and oil over a medium-low heat in a large, heavy-based pan. Fry the bacon for 3 minutes, then add the anchovies to the pan and sizzle until they're falling apart. Add the onion and cook for 5 minutes before throwing in the carrots and celery. Cover with a lid, turn the heat down and cook, stirring occasionally, for 10 minutes.

Once all this has had a chance to soften a little, add the beef and pork mince, turn up the heat and cook for a few minutes until browned. Pour in the wine and leave to simmer until the sauce no longer smells boozy. Add the milk, tomatoes and nutmeg. Turn the heat to its lowest setting, cover the pan with a lid and cook for 2 hours, stirring every now and again to stop the meat catching on the bottom. This ought to cook to a thick sauce – not a soupy, tomatoey Bolognese but a meatier, heartier version. You can add a splash of water during the cooking time if the sauce is drying out, but take care not to overdo it.

When the sauce is nearly ready, heat a large pan of salted water for the pasta. Once it's boiling, add the pasta and cook until as soft or as al dente as you like it. Season the bolognese with plenty of salt and pepper, toss through the pasta and serve straight away with plenty of grated Parmesan.

Serves 8

25g butter

1 tablespoon olive oil

100g smoked bacon, diced

3 anchovy fillets, finely chopped

1 large onion, finely chopped

2 medium carrots, diced

1 celery stick, diced

250g beef mince

250g pork mince

250ml white wine

200ml full-fat milk

1 x 400g can chopped tomatoes

Pinch of ground nutmeg

750g spaghetti, linguine or tagliatelle

Salt and black pepper, to taste

Grated Parmesan, to serve

BEEF RENDANG

This Indonesian stew, rich with beef, coconut and spice, is one of my new favourite dishes. Over the course of a very long, slow cook, the sauce changes from a watery broth the colour of tan leather to a caramelised, burnt umber paste so thick that it clings stickily to the beef chunks. It's an amazing metamorphosis, making a dry, meaty curry, unlike the saucy kormas and so on that we're more used to. If this long cook is intimidating, bear in mind that the vast majority of this time is totally hands-off, leaving you free to watch *Gilmore Girls*, get on with chores or coursework or make phone calls while it simmers, and the smell of lemongrass, coconut and spice wafts temptingly through the house.

First, make the paste: prepare all of the ingredients and combine in the bowl of a food processor. Blend everything together until the paste is thick and gritty, but with no large chunks left.

Heat a few drops of the oil in a large, heavy-based pan and fry the beef chunks over a high heat. Cook for a couple of minutes, turning regularly, until the edges are browned. It's best to do this in batches to avoid overcrowding (and steaming) the beef in the pan.

Remove the browned beef from the pan and set aside. Add the rest of the oil of the pan, set over a medium-low heat and add the paste. Cook for 4–5 minutes, stirring continuously, until the paste is fragrant and sizzling. Add the browned meat, sugar, coconut milk and water and stir to combine. Bring to a simmer, then turn the heat down as low as it will go and cook, with the lid off and stirring occasionally, for 3–4 hours. When the rendang is ready, the sauce should be very thick, intensely dark and well reduced, while the meat should be so tender that it falls apart under your fork. Serve with plenty of steamed rice.

Serves 4–5

For the paste:

4 cloves garlic

7–8cm fresh ginger, peeled and thickly sliced

8 medium red chillies

6 shallots, halved

75g desiccated coconut

2 sticks fresh lemongrass, thickly sliced

1 teaspoon ground turmeric

1 teaspoon ground cinnamon

1 teaspoon salt

2 tablespoons vegetable oil

1kg stewing/casserole steak, cut into large chunks

2 tablespoons soft light or dark brown sugar

2 x 400ml cans coconut milk

250ml water

More recipes with beef:
Mystic Pizza, page 201

PORK

WINTER SPLIT PEA AND CHORIZO SOUP

GNOCCHI WITH BACON AND DILL

5 DINNERS WITH SAUSAGES

MEATBALLS WITH STICKY
BLACKBERRY-ANISE SAUCE

If asked, I'd say that I never really cook with pork. If you were to say 'pork' to me I'd think of heavy gammon steaks and Homer Simpson-style pork chops, pork crackling and even a listicle I once read online about hams that look like politicians, and I'd answer confidently that I don't much like pork, and that I rarely buy it or cook it. But then I remember the bacon that I have some mornings, fried until it's spitting hot then slapped between two slices of cheap white bread. I might also remember the hot chorizo I tossed through a pile of kale, or the sausages baked in feather-light batter, the salami I shredded through my pasta or the meatballs I drowned in sweet berry jam, and I'd have to eat my words.

There's something about pork's sweet, mild saltiness, especially when cured, that means it doesn't take much of it to transform a meal. A little bacon, for instance, can turn a midweek storecupboard soup into a meal fit for queens. And in whatever guise you use it, whether mince, ham, bacon or sausage, it's also a great carrier for other flavours – think dried herbs such as thyme or sage, spicy mustard seeds, black pepper, cloves and sweet honey notes.

WINTER SPLIT PEA AND CHORIZO SOUP

The chorizo in this hearty winter soup infuses the whole thing with the gentle warmth of paprika, and adds a decidedly indulgent dimension to an otherwise frugal meal. A long simmer is crucial to cook, soften and eventually break down the split peas – it's this process that makes this a thick pea soup, rather than a watery, bitty broth with peas. I use half-strength stock here because the chorizo adds so much salt.

Heat the oil in a very large, heavy-based pan and add the onion, garlic, tomatoes and two-thirds of the diced chorizo. Cook over a medium-low heat for 10 minutes, stirring occasionally, until the tomatoes are very soft and the chorizo is fragrant.

Add the split peas, dried oregano and bay leaves, then pour in the stock and stir to combine. Bring to a bubble then leave to simmer over a low heat for 1½ hours, or until the soup is thick and the split peas are mushy. Top up with a little more water if the soup gets too thick, and stir every 20 minutes or so to prevent it sticking at the bottom of the pan.

When the soup is ready, fry the remaining chorizo in a drop of oil over a medium-high heat for 2–3 minutes until sizzling. Season the soup with a little salt and plenty of black pepper, then serve in deep bowls with a sprinkling of the fried chorizo on top.

Serves 4

2 tablespoons olive oil

1 large onion, finely chopped

3 cloves garlic, crushed

6 tomatoes, diced

150g cooking chorizo, diced

450g yellow split peas

2 teaspoons dried oregano

2 bay leaves

2 litres weak vegetable or
   chicken stock

Salt and black pepper,
   to taste

GNOCCHI WITH BACON AND DILL

Pork and celery work well together, and it shows in this simple gnocchi dish. Here, the celery's punch is tempered with cream, for a soothing earthiness that sits nicely alongside the salty bacon. Meanwhile, dill – by all accounts a divisive herb, as polarising as Marmite, Wes Anderson, Kanye – lifts the whole meal with its clean, rather medicinal, freshness. If you can't stand dill, use parsley instead, but do be generous with it, and don't scrimp on the lemon zest.

Set a pan of salted water to boil for the gnocchi. While the water heats, add a little oil to a large frying pan over a low heat and, once the pan is hot, cook the diced celery for 10 minutes, or until slightly softened. Add the bacon and continue frying for a further 2–3 minutes, then stir in the mustard.

Cook the gnocchi for 2 minutes in the boiling water (or follow the packet instructions) then immediately drain and add to the frying pan with the cooked celery and bacon. Stir everything together over a low heat with the butter, cream, lemon zest and dill. As soon as everything's combined, season generously with coarsely ground black pepper and a little salt and serve immediately.

Serves 4

Olive oil, for frying

5 celery sticks, finely diced

8 thick-cut unsmoked bacon rashers, diced

2 teaspoons wholegrain mustard

750g fresh gnocchi

50g butter

200ml single cream

Zest of 2 lemons

Bunch of dill, roughly chopped

Salt and black pepper, to taste

5 DINNERS WITH SAUSAGES

There are so many warnings at the moment about the perils of processed meat that sausages seem to have fallen out of favour. It seems a terrible shame, though, when it's meat like this – cheap, easy to cook, generously calorific – that plays such an important role in normal people's day-to-day diets. We can't all afford sirloin steaks or corn-fed chickens for dinner every day, and sausages are a cheap way of getting meat on the table when the budget is tight. Obviously it's worth getting the best quality sausages you can, but I don't think nutrition should be an all or nothing situation, and a couple of bangers every so often should be a meal to relish – not something to fear. Here are five easy, inexpensive, filling meals that you can make from a simple pack of sausages.

STUFFED PORTOBELLO MUSHROOMS WITH ALMOND AND GARLIC

Mushrooms, especially big portobello ones, have a natural meatiness of their own, so it's no surprise that they pair well with a sausagemeat stuffing. Make sure you use plenty of parsley to keep the flavour fresh.

Preheat the oven to 200°C/fan 180°C/gas mark 6 and lightly grease a large baking tray. Carefully tug out the stems of the mushrooms, finely chop them and place in a large mixing bowl. Arrange the mushrooms cup side up on the baking tray.

Melt the butter with a splash of oil over a low heat, then fry the shallots for 10 minutes, until tender. Add the garlic and cook for a further 2 minutes. Add this fragrant, buttery mixture to the chopped mushroom stalks in the mixing bowl then stir in a little over three-quarters of the breadcrumbs. Strip the sausage casing from the sausages, then add the meat filling to the mixing bowl along with the almonds and parsley. Stir to combine.

Divide this mixture between the prepared mushrooms and scatter the remaining breadcrumbs on top. Bake for 35–40 minutes, until the meat is cooked through and the mushrooms are perfectly tender.

Serves 4

8 portobello mushrooms

2 tablespoons butter

Splash of olive oil

4 shallots, finely chopped

2 cloves garlic, finely chopped

250g white breadcrumbs (10 slices, crusts removed)

6 good-quality pork sausages

50g almonds, roughly chopped

Large handful of parsley leaves, finely chopped

COMFORTING SAUSAGE AND POTATO PIE

Throw a few broccoli florets, some sliced mushrooms or a handful of frozen peas into the filling here if you want to shake things up, but I quite like the comforting creaminess of the pie just as it is, saving the veg for on the side.

Preheat the oven to 200°C/fan 180°C/gas mark 6. Cook the potatoes in boiling salted water for 10–15 minutes, or until you can easily pierce them with a fork. Drain and set aside.

While the potatoes cook, fry the onion and sausages in the oil over a medium-low heat, turning the sausages often and stirring the onion slices as you go. Fry for 10 minutes or so – just long enough to slightly soften the onion and to cook the sausages.

Set aside the cooked sausages and onion, then pour the chicken stock and cream into the frying pan. Set the pan back over the heat and deglaze it, scraping up any sausage scraps and letting the fat from the meat flavour the stock and cream. Whisk in the mustard and season, then bring to a simmer.

Slice the sausages into 3cm chunks and scatter into the baking dish with the potatoes and onion. Pour over the creamy stock, then roll out the puff pastry, drape it over the top of the dish and trim to size, pressing around the edges to seal. Score a hole in the pastry lid for the steam to escape and bake for 30 minutes until puffed and golden.

Serves 4

500g new potatoes, scrubbed and quartered

1 tablespoon olive oil

1 red onion, sliced

4 good-quality sausages

150ml chicken stock

150ml double cream

2 teaspoons wholegrain mustard

250g bought puff pastry

Salt and black pepper, to taste

15x22cm baking dish or a deep ceramic pie dish roughly that size

SAUSAGES WITH ORECCHIETTE, FENNEL AND PEPPER

This sausage and pasta dish is a delightful mix of colours, flavours and textures, with salty meat, sweet peppers and the aniseed lightness of fennel seeds. If you don't like aniseed flavours, swap in mustard seeds (or a little wholegrain mustard) in place of the fennel seeds.

Set a pan of water on to boil. While the water heats, very thinly slice the onions and peppers.

Warm the oil in a large, heavy-based pan over a low heat then add the sliced onions and peppers with the fennel seeds. Stir to combine, then cover with a lid and leave to cook gently – stirring every 5 minutes or so – for 20–25 minutes, or until the veg has cooked down to soft ribbons.

Meanwhile, salt the boiling water and cook the pasta to your liking. Fry or grill the chipolatas until browned and cooked through.

Once all the components are ready, slice the chipolatas into fat coins using a sharp knife. Toss the veg and sausages through the cooked, drained pasta, and season with a little salt and a very generous grinding of black pepper.

Serves 4

2 onions

4 red peppers

5 tablespoons olive oil

2 teaspoons fennel seeds

325g orecchiette, conchiglie, penne or other smallish pasta

12 chipolata sausages

Salt and black pepper, to taste

TOAD IN THE HOLE

The key to a good rise with toad in the hole is to get the pan or oven dish, and the oil in it, scorching hot before you add the batter, and then to get it into the oven as quickly as possible afterwards. A perfect toad also needs a little attention when it comes to cooking the sausages. If you add them straight to the batter in the pan, they'll emerge pallid and soft, no matter how fiercely you bake them. To avoid any sad sausages, I fry mine briefly before baking, crisping the skins for a richer flavour and a deep brown shine to contrast with the creamy batter around them.

Preheat the oven to 220°C/fan 200°C/gas mark 7 and have your roasting dish to hand.

Whisk together the eggs and flour in a large bowl to get a thick paste. Gradually add the milk and water, whisking all the while, until the batter is smooth and thin. Leave the batter to rest for 10–15 minutes while the oven comes to temperature.

Fry the sausages in a drop of oil for a couple of minutes on each side, until browned all over, then set aside.

Place the roasting dish in the preheated oven until searing hot, then pour in the oil and return to the oven for a couple of minutes. The oil should be hot enough that the batter sizzles as it hits it, but not so hot that it smokes and burns. Quickly pour the rested batter into the hot, oiled dish and arrange the fried sausages in it however they'll fit. Bake for 20 minutes, then reduce the oven temperature to 200°C/fan 180°C/gas mark 6 and cook for a further 20–25 minutes, until the batter has risen and is browned and crisp. Serve straight away with greens and gravy.

Serves 6
4 large eggs
175g plain flour
125ml milk
125ml water
12 Cumberland sausages
2 tablespoons vegetable oil

20x30cm roasting dish

SPICY SAUSAGE AND CANNELLINI BEAN CASSEROLE

This is my version of an indulgent Sunday lunch: a rich, spicy, bean-packed stew, as simple as it is delicious. It's perfect for those times when you need a big crowd-pleasing meal but can't face the fuss and mess of a full roast dinner.

Preheat the oven to 160°C/fan 140°C/gas mark 3.

Fry the bacon in a large, ovenproof pan or casserole over a low heat, then add the oil, onion and peppers. Gently cook for 15 minutes, partially covered with a lid, until the peppers are well softened.

Meanwhile, fry the sausages in a separate pan over a medium heat for 5 minutes or so. Turn them regularly so that their skins brown all over, but don't worry about cooking them through at this stage.

Add the garlic, brown sugar, paprika, oregano, cayenne and tomato purée to the casserole and fry for a further minute or two. Next, pour in the wine and simmer for 3–5 minutes to evaporate the alcohol (you can use extra stock in place of the wine if you prefer). Add the chopped tomatoes, drained beans, stock and the browned sausages and season with salt and pepper.

Place a lid on the pan and cook in the oven for 1–1¼ hours, but give it longer it you have the time – the flavour will only intensify the longer it has. Serve with mash or soft polenta.

Serves 4

75g smoked streaky bacon, diced

1 tablespoon olive oil

1 large onion, finely sliced

2 red or yellow peppers, sliced

12 chipolata sausages or 8 fat butcher's sausages

2 cloves garlic, finely chopped

2 teaspoons soft dark brown sugar

1 teaspoon hot paprika

1 teaspoon dried oregano

½ teaspoon cayenne pepper

1 tablespoon tomato purée

125ml dry white wine

1 x 400g can chopped tomatoes

1 x 400g can cannellini or haricot beans, drained

200ml chicken or vegetable stock

Salt and black pepper, to taste

MEATBALLS WITH STICKY BLACKBERRY-ANISE SAUCE

You need something fruity to balance the comforting heft of these meatballs. Usually it'd be a redcurrant or lingonberry sauce, but I've opted for something a little darker: an inky blackberry sauce, spiked with anise for a gentle liquorice sweetness. You can make a sauce with a little beef stock and double cream, too, if you really want to go all out, but I don't think these meatballs need it. Glazed with dark blackberry and served with buttery mash, this is a comfort food dream without any overwhelming richness.

First, prepare the blackberry sauce. Heat all the sauce ingredients in a small pan and simmer for 15 minutes, crushing the blackberries under the back of a spoon as it cooks. When the mixture is syrupy, strain out the blackberry seeds through a fine mesh sieve. Set the strained mixture back over the heat and simmer for 5–10 minutes, until sticky and thicker. Leave to cool and turn jammy, then add a little more water if the sauce is too sticky, or place back over the heat for a few minutes if it's not quite thick enough. Set aside while you prepare the meatballs, re-warming it when the rest of the dish is ready.

Combine all the meatball ingredients except the oil in a large bowl, and work together using your hands.

Heat a little oil in a large frying pan. Shape the meatball mixture into 32 small balls and cook them over a high heat for 3 minutes, turning frequently. Reduce the heat to medium-low and cook for a further 10–12 minutes, until the meatballs are cooked through.

Serve with the blackberry sauce – you can toss this through the meatballs in the pan, with a splash of water, if you want to glaze them all over – and heaps of smooth mash.

Makes 32, serving 4

For the sauce:

350g blackberries

225g caster sugar

50ml water

3 star anise

1 dried bay leaf

2 teaspoons red wine vinegar

For the meatballs:

250g pork mince

250g beef mince

50g white breadcrumbs

2 shallots or ½ onion, finely chopped

2 teaspoons dried thyme

½ teaspoon nutmeg

½ teaspoon salt

75ml milk

Oil, for frying

More recipes with pork:
Caldo Verde, page 42
Hot Mustard and Bramley Apple Sausage Rolls, page 114
Chorizo Burgers, page 245
Coffee Bourbon Glazed Ribs, page 343

FISH

MAPLE SOY GLAZED SALMON

CATALAN FISH STEW

BREAKFAST KEDGEREE

MILD COCONUT FISH CURRY

CIDER-SPIKED FISH PIE

ROSEMARY AND OLIVE HAKE
WITH CHERRY TOMATOES

Apart from fish fingers and the occasional piece of fish-shop battered cod, I never ate much fish or seafood growing up, so the last few years – since I left home and started cooking for myself – have been a steep learning curve. I started at the deep end with my university housemates, in a tiny Japanese restaurant in north London, where I tried my first sushi and fell in love with the fat chunks of salmon sashimi, as soft and as rich as butter, marbled with bright white fat. Slowly I learned to love whole sea bass baked with herbs, fillets of haddock in creamy sauce and even the oily, fishy taste of mackerel, served with sharp rhubarb. More recently, I gagged on my first ever oyster (I'll try again, in due course) and surprised myself by becoming an unlikely convert to mussels, clams and huge king prawns tossed through garlicky linguine. As with every chapter in this book, I can't possibly hope to cover everything in this short section. You can see the recipes over the next few pages as an entry point, though, into cooking with fish: a few ideas for using easily available fish in simple, filling meals – no scary sea creatures, no oysters, no fuss.

MAPLE SOY GLAZED SALMON

Sweet maple syrup really sets off the saltiness of the soy sauce glaze – a riff on a traditional teriyaki mixture – in this salmon recipe. Because there's so much sugar in the sauce, it's important to let it simmer and thicken by itself before you add it to the salmon pan; if you pour the glaze into the frying pan while it's still very runny, it'll burn and smoke before it has a chance to thicken.

Whisk together all the ingredients for the glaze.

Heat a little oil in a heavy-based, non-stick frying pan, then fry the salmon fillets for 3–4 minutes each side, depending on their thickness, until cooked through. Meanwhile, simmer the glaze in a small pan for a few minutes, until reduced and syrupy.

Once the salmon is nearly cooked and the glaze is ready, pour the glaze into the frying pan over the fish. Finish cooking the salmon, spooning the glaze over the fillets to coat them, then serve straight away with stir-fried greens (I used pak choi), drizzling over any excess glaze when you dish it up. Steam plenty of rice for on the side.

Serves 4

For the glaze:

Juice of 1 lime

4 tablespoons dark soy sauce

3 tablespoons maple syrup

3 tablespoons mirin

1 clove garlic, crushed

¼ teaspoon crushed chillies

4cm fresh ginger, peeled and grated

Vegetable oil, for frying

4 salmon fillets

CATALAN FISH STEW

What makes this fish stew special is the ground almond, garlic and paprika mixture that adds a rich, nutty depth to the sauce and gives it body. Once you add the fish to this stew, the clock starts ticking and you'll need to have it on the table within 10 minutes or so in order to taste it at its best. If you want to prepare this in advance, it's best to just make the broth and hold off adding the fish and prawns until the last minute when you're nearly ready to serve.

Preheat the oven to 180°C/fan 160°C/gas mark 4. Once the oven is hot, spread the almonds across a baking tray and roast for 10–12 minutes, until they're a couple of shades darker and sizzling hot. Take care not to burn them, but don't whisk them out of the oven before they've had a chance to toast properly, because it's this that gives them their flavour.

While the almonds cook, prepare the tomatoes. Cut out the stems, score an X on the bottom of each one and place in a bowl or pan of boiling water for a minute or two, or until their skins start to split. Transfer the tomatoes to a bowl of cold water for another couple of minutes then peel off their skins. Cut the peeled tomatoes into dice.

Heat the oil in a large pan, add the onions and cook over a low heat for 15 minutes. Either with a pestle and mortar or in a food processor, pound or blitz the toasted almonds with the garlic and paprika, until no lumps remain. Add the almond mixture, tomato purée, sugar and saffron to the softened onions and cook for a couple of minutes, stirring all the while.

Add the diced tomatoes to the pan and cook over a low heat for 10 minutes, until the tomatoes are mushy. Add the white wine and cook for a further 3–5 minutes to evaporate the alcohol. Now add the fish stock, stir, and leave to simmer for 15–20 minutes to allow the flavours to blend.

Add the cod, simmering for 4–5 minutes to cook it through. A minute or two before the end of the cooking time, stir in the cooked prawns to heat them through. Finally, add the chopped parsley and serve with plenty of crusty bread.

Serves 4, generously

75g blanched almonds

10 ripe tomatoes

3 tablespoons olive oil

2 small onions, finely chopped

4 cloves garlic

2 teaspoons paprika

2 tablespoons tomato purée

2 teaspoons caster or granulated sugar

Pinch of saffron threads

350ml dry white wine

750ml fish stock

4 cod fillets, about 500g, cut into medium chunks

300g cooked, peeled prawns

Handful of parsley, finely chopped

BREAKFAST KEDGEREE

This could be the salty, moreish, nourishing hangover breakfast from heaven, if only it were a little simpler. Though it's not a tricky dish to master, there are a few components – egg, rice, fish – to prepare separately, which can be difficult for a groggy mind to handle. Save this for calmer mornings, then, when you've got a little time to spare and an appetite for something great.

Melt the butter in a large, heavy-based pan over a low heat. Fry the spring onions with the cardamom, bay leaves, curry powder and cinnamon for 5 minutes or so, then add the rice and crumble in the stock cube. Stir to coat the rice with the butter, add the cold water, and increase the heat to bring to a simmer.

Meanwhile, place the eggs in a small pan of cold water and set over a high heat. Once the water reaches the boil, immediately turn off the heat and cover the pan with a lid. Leave the eggs to sit for 6–7 minutes, then dunk in cold water and peel.

Once the rice has begun to simmer, turn the heat as low as possible and cover the pan with a tight-fitting lid. Leave to cook for 15 minutes, then – leaving the lid on – turn off the heat and let it sit for a further 5 minutes.

While the rice cooks and then rests, poach the fish in a pan of barely simmering water for 4–5 minutes. Remove the fish then cook the peas for a couple of minutes in the same water.

To serve, break the fish fillets into large chunks and stir through the rice along with the peas. Season the rice to taste with a little salt, but remember that the fish chunks will impart their own saline tang, so don't overdo it. Cut the eggs into quarters. Divide the rice between four bowls, topping each one with a couple of lemon wedges, segments of boiled egg and a sprinkling of parsley.

Serves 4

50g butter

4 spring onions, sliced

4 cardamom pods, crushed

2 bay leaves

1½ tablespoons mild curry powder

¼ teaspoon ground cinnamon

250g basmati rice, thoroughly rinsed and drained

½ vegetable stock cube

350ml cold water

4 eggs

300g smoked haddock, cod or river cobbler

75g frozen peas

Salt, to taste

1 lemon, cut into wedges

Handful of fresh parsley, roughly chopped

MILD COCONUT FISH CURRY

Sometimes a dish isn't about one, or two, or even a handful of standout flavours, but about the magic that happens when several elements – a whisper of cardamom, a hint of ginger heat, a trace of bay – merge and come together as one. That's exactly what happens in this Goan fish curry, where the long ingredients list, far from creating a racket of competing flavours, simmers away to a beautifully smooth coconut sauce that's sweet, rich, tangy and hot in perfect balance.

Tamarind paste is what traditionally gives this South Indian curry a light sourness, and you can find it in most large supermarkets. If you can't get hold of it, though, just use lemon juice to deliver that edge.

Toast the turmeric, cumin, mustard seeds, ground coriander and crushed chilli in a dry frying pan over a medium-low heat for a minute or two, stirring continuously. Whisk the pan off the heat as soon as the mustard seeds start to pop and the spices are fragrant.

Heat the oil in a medium pan over a low heat, and fry the onion for 10 minutes until slightly softened. Add the spice mix, garlic, green chillies, ginger, cardamom, bay leaves and tomato purée and cook for a further couple of minutes before throwing in the chopped tomatoes. Sizzle for 2–3 minutes, then add the coconut milk and 100–150ml water and simmer, with the lid off, for 15–25 minutes (the longer you give it, the more intense the flavour will be).

Once the sauce has reduced, add the fish and cook for a further 4–5 minutes over a low heat – the sauce should be barely bubbling. Once the fish is cooked through, stir in the tamarind paste or lemon juice and season to taste. Sprinkle with chopped coriander and serve with rice.

Serves 4

2 teaspoons ground turmeric

2 teaspoons ground cumin

2 teaspoons mustard seeds

1 teaspoon ground coriander

¼–½ teaspoon crushed dried chilli

4 tablespoons olive or vegetable oil

1 onion, finely chopped

4 cloves garlic, finely chopped

2 medium green chillies, deseeded and finely chopped

5cm fresh ginger, grated

3 cardamom pods, split

2 bay leaves

3 tablespoons tomato purée

1 x 400g can chopped tomatoes

1 x 400ml can coconut milk

500g haddock, tilapia, or river cobbler fillet, cut into chunks

1 tablespoon tamarind paste or juice of 1 lemon

Small handful of coriander leaves, coarsely chopped

Salt and black pepper, to taste

CIDER-SPIKED FISH PIE

Typically the crisp fruitiness of cider would be too much alongside white fish, but here – with the calming influence of a creamy sauce and the richness of smoked haddock– it works perfectly to lighten this fish pie and to echo the gentle tang of the Cheddar cheese on top. Poaching the fish before it goes in the oven might seem like overkill, but it makes a huge difference to the final dish when the fish has that chance to infuse the milk with its flavour. As long as you don't give the pie excessively long in the oven, the fish should remain perfectly tender and moist, despite being twice-cooked.

Preheat the oven to 200°C/fan 180°C/gas mark 6.

Place the potato chunks in a pan of cold, salted water. Bring to the boil and cook until tender. Once ready, mash with the butter and milk and season generously.

While the potatoes cook, heat the milk for the filling until it's nearly boiling and cut the fish into chunks. Poach the fish in the hot milk over a very low heat for 3–4 minutes (the fish needn't be cooked through at this point) then strain the milk into a separate bowl and put the fish aside for a moment.

Melt the butter over a low heat then add the flour. Leave to sizzle for a couple of minutes, stirring all the while, then slowly whisk in the cider until you're left with a smooth paste. Let it bubble for a minute then gradually add the poaching milk. Stir over the heat until the sauce is smooth and slightly thickened, then add 75g of the grated Cheddar, the fish chunks and peas.

Pour the filling into the oven dish and top with the mashed potato. Sprinkle over the remaining Cheddar and bake for 20–25 minutes, until the mash is golden and crisp on top.

Serves 4

For the potato topping:

750g floury potatoes, such as Maris Piper, peeled and cut into large chunks

50g salted butter

50ml milk

Salt and black pepper, to taste

For the filling:

350ml full-fat milk

250g cod fillet

250g smoked haddock

30g salted butter

3 tablespoons plain flour

150ml dry cider

125g mild Cheddar, grated

150g frozen peas

1.5–2 litre oven dish

ROSEMARY AND OLIVE HAKE WITH CHERRY TOMATOES

This dish shows that with a little time and some careful cooking, you can turn just a handful of simple ingredients into a flavourful one-pot meal. Because it's braised in the sticky tomato mixture, the hake stays perfectly moist and tender, soaking up the rosemary and garlic aromas as it cooks. Serve with ciabatta to absorb the tomato juices.

Heat the olive oil in a large, deep frying pan over a medium heat. A high-sided pan will do if you don't have a frying pan large enough. Fry the garlic and whole rosemary sprigs for a minute or two, until fragrant but not browning. Add the cherry tomatoes and cook over a low heat for 15 minutes, stirring occasionally.

Add the olives, put a lid on the pan, and cook for 15 minutes more until the tomatoes are meltingly soft. Season the tomato mixture to taste then set the hake fillets in the pan, nestling them down among the veg. Put the lid back on and cook for 6–8 minutes, until the fish is cooked through and flakes under a fork.

Serves 4

75ml olive oil

4 cloves garlic, thinly sliced

4 sprigs of rosemary

1kg cherry tomatoes

125g Kalamata olives, pitted and halved

4 skinless and boneless hake fillets (you can also use cod)

Salt and black pepper, to taste

More recipes with fish and seafood:
Smoked Mackerel Potato Rösti with Sour Cream and Lemon, page 81
Deep-fried Anchovy-stuffed Sage Leaves, page 95
Herb-packed Fishcakes with Hot Lemon Wedges, page 105
Crisp Fried Sea Bass with Coconut Rice and Mango, page 125
Zesty Chilli Prawn Noodles, page 138
Herbed Salmon and Ricotta Quiche, page 203
All-in-one Basil Cod with Potatoes and Green Lentils, page 295

STORE-CUPBOARD

LENTILS AND PULSES

5 DINNERS WITH A CAN OF CHICKPEAS

HOT AND SOUR RED LENTIL SOUP

LEMONY GREEN LENTIL SOUP

FAMILY VEGAN CHILLI

KALE, BORLOTTI BEAN AND
PUMPKIN SEED ENCHILADAS

ALL-IN-ONE BASIL COD WITH
POTATOES AND GREEN LENTILS

I have a survival kit. It's not packed up neat in a first-aid tin or tucked into my backpack, it's strewn through the debris of my flat – in my cupboards, littered over my bedroom floor, on laptop drives and in kitchen drawers. When anxiety flares up, these are the things that don't just keep me afloat, but raise me higher: a pot of glitter nail varnish, thick with sparkle flecks; *Bridget Jones's Diary* on a scuffed DVD; a stack of Nigel Slater books, so gleeful in their food-positivity that they can rouse my appetite even when I'm sick with tiredness; a framed photo of Laverne Cox, radiant with a milkshake; a small archive of inspirational Harry Styles hairstyle pictures.

Maybe less exciting but just as invaluable are the cans of chickpeas and the packets of red lentils, that I always have on standby in the kitchen cupboard. In times of stress or apathy, these are the only foods I can bear to cook – thick lentil soup, ten-minute chickpea suppers and warm salads – both nourishing and gratifyingly hearty, happy to be left alone bubbling on the stove while I get the duvet set up on the sofa and that worn-out Bridget Jones disc in the DVD player. If you're someone who might benefit from this kind of easy comfort food – and indeed the cathartic rhythms of cooking it – you should certainly work a few simple lentil and pulse recipes into your weeknight dinner repertoire. Apart from being protein-packed, versatile and easy to prepare, these are the kind of storecupboard staples that'll save your bacon on those long days when you can't even summon the strength to amble to the shop.

5 DINNERS WITH A CAN OF CHICKPEAS

There was a time when I was still at university, skint and lazy, when I'd eat chickpeas from the can for dinner. These days, though, things have changed, and I don't believe in feeding myself anything that I wouldn't be happy to serve up to the people I love most; if you wouldn't serve Nicki Minaj cold chickpeas and ketchup, don't eat it yourself. Not every meal has to be extravagant, but you owe it to yourself to exercise a little self-care. Eating on a budget needn't mean that you can't eat like a queen, especially when you let chickpeas save the day – no pricey cuts of meat, no lengthy cooking times or fiddly components, only a frugal feast.

CHORIZO AND CHICKPEAS WITH COD

I make this as a reasonably dry dish, but you can make it saucier by using a whole 400g can of chopped tomatoes rather than the 200g called for here.

Fry the chorizo over a medium-low heat until it releases its oils, then add the garlic and cook for a further minute or two.

Add the chopped tomatoes, chickpeas, white wine (or a little water, if you don't have an open bottle), smoked paprika, chilli and plenty of salt and pepper. Simmer for a couple of minutes over a low heat, crushing some of the chickpeas under a fork while it cooks. Meanwhile, fry the two cod fillets in a little oil over a medium heat, for 2 minutes or so on each side. At the last minute, add the spinach to the chickpea mixture and cook until wilted. Serve the cod on a bed of the chickpeas and chorizo.

Serves 2

100g cooking chorizo, in slices as thick as a £1 coin

1 clove garlic, finely sliced

200g canned chopped tomatoes

1 x 400g can chickpeas, rinsed and drained

2 tablespoons dry white wine

½ teaspoon smoked paprika

¼ teaspoon crushed chillies

2 boneless cod fillets, roughly 125g each

Olive oil, for frying

75g spinach

Salt and black pepper, to taste

GARLIC AND CHILLI CHICKPEA PASTA

My parents used to make this all the time as a super-quick schoolnight supper. It's spectacularly simple, and that's the joy of it: a no-fuss, no-sauce pasta dish that you can bring together from cupboard to plate in barely 20 minutes. Tweak the amount of chilli and cheese depending on whether you want a clean, fiery pasta or a cheesier comfort dinner. Whatever you do, though, don't skimp on the garlic, which brings this whole meal alive with its fragrant heat.

Boil the pasta in well-salted water until it's cooked to your taste.

Meanwhile, heat the oil in a frying pan over a medium-low heat and fry the garlic and chilli for 1–2 minutes, until the garlic is beginning to turn golden. Immediately add the chickpeas and plenty of salt and pepper, and cook for a further couple of minutes to heat the chickpeas through.

Drain the pasta, reserving a little of the cooking water, and add it to the pan with the chickpeas. Stir together over a low heat with a couple of tablespoons of the reserved water and the butter. Season well and serve straight away with shaved Parmesan.

Serves 2

175g spaghetti or linguine, broken into shorter shards

2 tablespoons good-quality olive oil

2 cloves garlic, thinly sliced

¼ teaspoon crushed chillies

1 x 400g can chickpeas, rinsed and drained

1 tablespoon butter

Shaved Parmesan, to serve

Salt and black pepper, to taste

VEGETABLE-PACKED CHICKPEA AND ORZO MINESTRONE

Chickpeas lend body to this already filling soup, though you could always throw in a little chopped bacon or chorizo for extra protein. It's so easy to make a big batch of this and then to portion and chill or freeze it, so it's often something I make on a Sunday evening to last me a week of packed lunches.

Heat the oil in a large pan, add the onions and fry over a low heat for 15 minutes, stirring regularly, until the onions have softened. Add the garlic, celery, carrot and pepper and cook for a further 10 minutes, partially covered by a lid.

Pour in the chopped tomatoes and chickpeas with the boiling water, then stir in the orzo. Simmer for 20 minutes, stirring a couple of times to stop the orzo sticking to the bottom. Add the peas 3 minutes before the end of the cooking time and season with salt and black pepper.

Serve in deep bowls and top each portion with a dollop of pesto and a few basil leaves scattered on top.

Serves 3–4

2 tablespoons olive oil

1 onion, finely chopped

2 cloves garlic, finely chopped

2 sticks celery, diced

2 carrots, diced

1 yellow or orange pepper, diced

1 x 400g can chopped tomatoes

1 x 400g can chickpeas, rinsed and drained

750ml boiling water

50g orzo or small soup pasta

50g frozen peas

Salt and black pepper, to taste

2 tablespoons red pesto, to serve

Handful of basil leaves, to serve

SAFFRON CHICKPEA PILAF

Buttery, saffron-scented rice is at the heart of this pilaf, but it's the earthy, spiced chickpeas that make this dish a meal in its own right. The method's really easy – just fry onion and spices, add the chickpeas and rice, top up with water and cook until the rice is tender – but make sure you don't surrender to temptation and prematurely lift the lid: if you do, you'll release all the steam that the rice needs in order to cook to fluffy perfection.

Preheat the oven to 180°C/fan 160°C/gas mark 4, then toast the flaked almonds on a baking tray for 6–8 minutes, until golden. Set aside to cool.

Melt the butter in a heavy-based pan over a low heat, then add the onion, coriander seeds, cinnamon, cardamom, crushed chillies and saffron and fry for 15 minutes, until the onion is very soft. Stir in the chickpeas, peas and lemon zest. Add the rice with plenty of salt, stir to coat the rice with the butter, then add the water and bring to a boil.

As soon as the mixture starts to bubble, reduce to the lowest heat, put a lid on the pan and cook for 15 minutes. Take the pan off the heat (leaving the lid on!) and leave to sit and steam for 10 minutes, so the rice can finish cooking. Wilt the spinach in a little boiling water in a pan or heatproof bowl. Fluff the rice with a fork, mix in the wilted and drained spinach, toasted flaked almonds, pistachios and herbs and serve immediately.

Serves 2–3

25g flaked almonds

50g salted butter

1 onion, finely chopped

1 teaspoon coriander seeds, roughly crushed

1 cinnamon stick or ½ teaspoon ground cinnamon

3 cardamom pods, crushed

Between a pinch and ¼ teaspoon crushed chillies

Generous pinch of saffron threads

1 x 400g can chickpeas, rinsed and drained

75g frozen peas

Zest of ½ lemon

125g basmati rice, thoroughly rinsed and drained

175ml cold water

75g spinach

25g pistachios, roughly chopped

Small handful of fresh parsley, roughly chopped

Small handful of fresh coriander, finely chopped

Salt, to taste

WARM SPICED CHICKPEA AND CARROT SALAD

Golden fried chunks of pitta bread bulk out the warm chickpeas in this comforting salad. Serve as it is or with a mound of seasoned, herb-strewn couscous if you're very hungry.

Heat half of the oil in a medium pan, add the onion and cook for 10–15 minutes over a low heat. Add the garlic, ground coriander, oregano, paprika and nutmeg and cook for a further 2 minutes or so before throwing in the carrots, chickpeas and stock. Put a lid on the pan and cook for 10 minutes, then remove the lid and leave to simmer until most of the liquid has evaporated.

While the chickpeas cook, heat the remaining oil in a frying pan and fry the pieces of pitta bread for 2–3 minutes, turning a couple of times, until golden and beginning to crisp. Once the chickpeas have cooked, let them cool a little then season with plenty of salt and pepper. Toss through the cooked pitta pieces, a tiny splash of white wine vinegar and the coriander leaves. Serve warm.

Serves 2

4 tablespoons olive oil

1 small onion, finely sliced

2 cloves garlic, sliced

1 teaspoon ground coriander

½ teaspoon dried oregano

½ teaspoon paprika

¼ teaspoon grated nutmeg

2 smallish carrots, cut into ¼cm-thick rounds

1 x 400g can chickpeas, rinsed and drained

200ml vegetable or chicken stock

1 pitta bread, torn into small pieces

Splash of white wine vinegar

Handful of fresh coriander leaves

Salt and black pepper, to taste

HOT AND SOUR RED LENTIL SOUP

A hazy idea for this recipe came to me several weeks before I actually managed to make a palatable version of it. I knew I wanted a fiery red lentil soup: the opposite of the kinds of gentle soups I've traditionally made (like the lemony green lentil soup in the next recipe); one hot enough to blast a creeping cold from my system and so hearty that it's a meal in itself. I tried versions with charred red peppers, others stained ochre with smoked paprika and a particularly nasty version speckled with flecks of red kidney bean skin. It took a good ten attempts before I managed to settle on this incarnation of the recipe, inspired by Thai tom yum soups, freshened with garlic, lemongrass and kaffir lime to soften the punch of the chilli. It was so worth the wait.

Heat the oil in a large pan and gently cook the tomatoes over a low heat for 3–4 minutes, until they begin to melt into a very soft mass.

Add the ginger, lime leaves, garlic, lemongrass and tomato purée and stir to blend everything together. Add the lentils along with the boiling water and simmer for 15 minutes, adding the chillies 5 minutes before the end of the cooking time. Stir in the lime juice at the last minute and season generously with salt.

Serves 4

2 tablespoons vegetable oil

6 tomatoes, diced

5cm fresh ginger, sliced

3 kaffir lime leaves

2 cloves garlic, sliced

1 stick lemongrass, bruised

2 tablespoons tomato purée

200g red lentils

1.25 litres boiling water

2 bird's eye chillies, thinly sliced

Juice of 2 limes

Salt, to taste

LEMONY GREEN LENTIL SOUP

This lemony soup goes to show that comfort food needn't be heavy to be soothing. Unlike red lentils, these smaller green lentils hold their shape when cooked, making for a soup that's light and clear with a clean, bright taste. It's the soup I turn to when, in a tangle of anxiety, illness or stress, I just need to be healed. The citrussy edge of chard pairs really nicely as an alternative to the spinach, if you can get hold of a bunch.

Heat the oil in a large, heavy-based pan over a medium-low heat, then add the onion, celery, carrots and dried herb. Sweat the vegetables gently for 15 minutes, partially covered, then add the garlic and cook for a further minute or two.

Stir in the lentils and stock, bring to the boil and simmer over a low heat for 30 minutes, or until the lentils are tender. When the soup is ready, stir in the spinach until wilted before removing the pan from the heat and adding the lemon juice. Serve immediately with a dollop of yoghurt and a drizzle of olive oil on top.

Serves 4 generously

2 tablespoons olive oil, plus extra for drizzling

1 onion, finely chopped

3 sticks celery, diced

2 carrots, diced

1 teaspoon dried thyme or oregano

2 cloves garlic, crushed

200g French green lentils (lentilles vertes)

1.2 litres vegetable stock

200g spinach or chard

Juice of 1 lemon

100g natural yoghurt

FAMILY VEGAN CHILLI

My dad used to make a version of this filling vegan chilli all the time for my three siblings and me. Because there's no chuck steak, mince, bacon or chorizo, it's a lot cheaper than meaty chilli recipes, and far easier to cobble together from whatever you have left in the storecupboard. I err on the side of mildness here, but you can of course add as much or as little chilli powder as you like.

Heat the oil in a large, heavy-based pan and cook the onion, carrots, celery and dried marjoram or oregano over a medium-low heat, covered with a lid, for 15 minutes. Stir every so often to stop the vegetables sticking to the pan.

Once the veg has started to sweat, add the ground cumin, paprika and chilli powder, before stirring in the red kidney beans, chopped tomatoes, rice, tomato ketchup and vegetable stock. Bring to a simmer, then turn down the heat and cook for 30–40 minutes, until the vegetables are tender and the sauce is reduced, thick and rich. It's really important that you stir the chilli regularly as it simmers, or the rice will sink and burn on the bottom of the pan. Top up with a little extra stock or water if the pan looks too dry.

Season with salt and black pepper and serve with steamed basmati rice, cornbread, or the Chilli Cornbread Pancakes on page 190.

Serves 4

3 tablespoons olive oil

1 onion, finely chopped

2 carrots, diced

2 celery sticks, diced

2 teaspoons dried marjoram or oregano

1 teaspoon ground cumin

½ teaspoon paprika

½–1 teaspoon hot chilli powder, to taste

2 x 400g cans red kidney beans, rinsed and drained

1 x 400g can chopped tomatoes

75g basmati rice, rinsed and drained

2 tablespoons tomato ketchup

750–850ml vegetable stock

Salt and black pepper, to taste

KALE, BORLOTTI BEAN AND PUMPKIN SEED ENCHILADAS

These enchiladas couldn't be further from the clichés of vegan food – mean-spirited, bland, soulless – that some old-fashioned foodies cling to. I was vegan for a year and I ate more creatively and more thoughtfully than ever: big soups and stews, homemade flapjacks and trays of chewy cookies, steaming puddings and hearty veg-packed pies. Though I eat meat and dairy now, there are still a few vegan dishes so good that I revisit them time and time again, not because of obligation or morality or health, but because they're delicious. These enchiladas, heavy with spiced veg, beans and seeds, and baked in a piquant chilli tomato sauce, are a case in point.

Preheat the oven to 180°C/fan 160°C/gas mark 4 and have a 20x30cm roasting tin or oven dish ready.

Heat half of the oil in a large pan, add the onions and soften over a low heat for 15 minutes. Add the garlic, cumin, paprika, oregano and chilli powder and cook for 2 minutes.

In a separate pan, heat the remaining oil and fry the courgettes for 8–10 minutes over a medium-low heat, until browned but not completely soft. Scoop half of the cooked onion mixture into the pan of courgettes once they're ready, then stir in the kale, borlotti beans, pumpkin seeds and half a mug of water. Cook for 5 minutes or so, until the kale has wilted and most of the water is gone. Season generously.

To the remaining onion mixture, add the chopped tomatoes and cook for 10 minutes over a low heat, then season with plenty of salt and pepper.

Divide the borlotti bean mixture between the six tortillas, scooping it into a sausage shape along the middle of each one. Fold the ends over to cover the tips of the filling, then roll each side over to wrap the vegetables safely inside. Pour a third of the tomato sauce mixture into the roasting dish and arrange the tortillas on top, placing them with their join facing downwards so that they don't unfurl. Spoon the remaining tomato sauce over the top and bake in the oven for 30 minutes, until sizzling.

Serves 6

4 tablespoons olive oil

2 onions, thinly sliced

4 cloves garlic, finely chopped

3 teaspoons ground cumin

2 teaspoons smoked paprika

2 teaspoons dried oregano

½ teaspoon hot chilli powder

2 small courgettes, cut into 2cm dice

150g kale, trimmed and roughly chopped

2 x 400g cans borlotti beans, rinsed and drained

50g pumpkin seeds

2 x 400g cans chopped tomatoes

6 wheat tortillas

Salt and black pepper, to taste

ALL-IN-ONE BASIL COD WITH POTATOES AND GREEN LENTILS

I came up with this recipe with my mum in mind: minimal prep work and hardly any washing up for a no-trauma weeknight dinner. The potatoes and lentils cook in the hot stock while the fish steams on top, so you'll need just one big oven pan or roasting dish to cook the whole meal – carb, fish and veg all in one. Use any kind of green lentils for this: I like the standard dull green kind, but the smaller, shinier French green lentils also work. As for the fish, though I've specified cod, haddock is a good alternative.

Preheat the oven to 200°C/fan 180°C/gas mark 6.

Scatter the potatoes and lentils into a 20x30cm roasting dish and dot roughly two-thirds of the pesto over the top. Pour the hot stock gently over everything, using only enough to just cover the potatoes and lentils, then bake for 35–40 minutes.

Spread the remaining pesto over the tops of the fish fillets. When the potatoes are tender, the lentils soft and most of the liquid evaporated, lay the fish on top of the bake and return to the oven for 5–10 minutes, depending on the thickness of your fish fillets. When the fish is ready, it should flake under a fork. Serve immediately, scooping up plenty of basil-scented lentil and potato with your fish.

Serves 4

500g baby potatoes, scrubbed and cut into 5mm slices

160g green lentils

175g green pesto

600–700ml hot vegetable stock

4 skinless and boneless cod fillets, each roughly 125g

More recipes with lentils and pulses:
Smoky Butternut Squash Stew with Chickpea Dumplings, page 66
Spicy Sausage and Cannellini Bean Casserole, page 263

NUTS AND SEEDS

HAZELNUT PORRIDGE

SEEDED WHOLEMEAL MUFFINS
WITH HONEY BUTTER

PRETZEL PEANUT BUTTER PIE

STICKY WALNUT
CINNAMON SWIRLS

HOMEMADE NUT BUTTER

SPICED ALMOND AND
LAMB FLATBREADS

We're not very good at cooking with nuts and seeds here in the UK. Apart from a packet of salted peanuts guzzled at the bar with a cold pint (certainly not to be sniffed at, but also not our most ambitious culinary pairing), they barely figure in our day-to-day cooking. We don't have the kind of heart-stopping peanut butter stews as you might find in West Africa (see page 231), or even the lightness of an almond picada scattered over a stew or casserole as in Spain (there's a fish stew recipe on page 270 that does just that). When I do see nuts and seeds showcased in recipes, it's often in a faddish way: think chia seeds thrown into muesli, breakfast bars and fruit bowls on some vogueish, expensive whim.

We can do better by nuts and seeds than bar snacks and health food. There are a thousand ways to work them into your cooking – both sweet and savoury – for flavour, body and bite, not least in baking. Because ground nuts have a high oil content and lack the elasticising gluten of flour, using them in cakes and breads will give a softer crumb; meanwhile try the textural contrast of a crust of crunchy seeds against the tenderness of a muffin, cupcake or bun, or even have a go at making your own nut butter.

HAZELNUT PORRIDGE

Somehow the roasted hazelnut in this porridge makes the whole dish feel sweeter and richer, though that's not stopped me from taking things a step further by serving with double cream and muscovado. If you can't get roasted ground hazelnuts in your local supermarket it's easy to make your own: toast blanched hazelnuts in a 180°C/fan 160°C/gas mark 4 oven for 10 minutes, leave to cool then pulse in a food processor or coffee grinder until the meal is very slightly coarser than the texture of ground almonds.

Combine all of the ingredients in a large, heavy-based pan and keep a close eye on it as it cooks over a medium heat. Once the mixture begins to simmer, turn the heat down to low and let the porridge cook and thicken for a further 2–3 minutes, stirring continuously.

Divide the porridge between four bowls and swirl through with teaspoons of dark brown sugar and, if the mood takes you, a drizzle of double cream.

Serves 4

200g jumbo rolled oats

100g roasted ground hazelnuts

850ml milk (semi-skimmed or full-fat works best)

400ml water

Pinch of salt

To serve:

Soft dark brown sugar

Double cream (optional)

SEEDED WHOLEMEAL MUFFINS WITH HONEY BUTTER

These sweet, nutty muffins are delicious as they are but they're even better served warm from the oven with homemade honey butter. You can make any flavoured butter this way: cinnamon, maple, honeycomb, chilli, herb or garlic.

Beat the butter until creamy then stir in the honey one tablespoon at a time. Mix well until the butter is perfectly smooth and then refrigerate until set. (If you want to serve the butter neatly, wrap it in cling film and press into a log shape when it's partly chilled before returning it to the fridge to set completely.)

Make the muffins while the honey butter sets. Preheat the oven to 180°C/fan 160°C/gas mark 4. Line the muffin tin with paper muffin cases. Whisk the oil, honey and eggs together in a large bowl. Stir the dry ingredients together in a separate bowl before adding to the egg mixture and stirring well to combine. Divide the batter between the paper cases in the muffin tin, taking care not to fill them to the brim. (Bake a few extra in a second batch if you're worried that yours will overflow in the oven.)

Bake for 20–25 minutes until well risen and springy to the touch. A small knife inserted into the centre of one of the cakes should emerge more or less clean. Leave to cool until they're just warm in the middle then eat, tearing each open and spreading on plenty of the honey butter.

Serves 12

For the honey butter:
100g salted butter, softened
2 tablespoons runny honey

For the muffins:
150ml sunflower or
  vegetable oil
150g runny honey
3 large eggs
125g plain flour
50g wholemeal flour
2 teaspoons baking powder
½ teaspoon ground cinnamon
100g seeds, such as
  sunflower, pumpkin, sesame
  and poppy

12-hole muffin tin

PRETZEL PEANUT BUTTER PIE

In New York there's a bakery called Momofuku Milk Bar, a city institution with a near cult following, known for its irreverently anti-minimalist cookies, pies and ice creams, in flavours such as cereal milk, compost and birthday cake. My favourite is the Candy Bar Pie, packed with nuts, caramel, pretzels and chocolate. This is a simplified version of that pie, toned down for making at home.

Preheat the oven to 180°C/fan 160°C/gas mark 4 and have your pie tin ready. I make mine in a smallish metal pie dish with sloping slides, roughly 16cm across at its base and 20cm wide at the rim – any tin with roughly these dimensions will work well. If you're using a bigger dish or perhaps an 18–20cm diameter round cake tin, make extra crust and filling to help the mixture go around. Grease the dish lightly with butter or a little oil.

Blitz the pretzels for the crust in a food processor or coffee grinder (or place in a sturdy freezer bag and bash with a rolling pin) until they're finely crushed, almost floury. Mix the pretzel dust with the sugar and flour then rub in the butter between your fingertips. Add enough milk to make the mixture slightly sticky so it'll hold together in clumps. Pack the mixture firmly into the base of the pie tin. Bake the pretzel crust for 13–15 minutes.

While the crust cools, prepare the filling. Combine the peanut butter, sugar, condensed milk and salt in a medium, heavy-based pan and set over a medium-high heat. Stir continuously, making sure you cover the whole of the base of the pan as you stir, as this sugar-rich mixture is prone to browning and burning if left to sit. Once the filling reaches the boil, cook for a further 3 minutes or so, until it has begun to thicken and has darkened a shade. Remove from the heat, stir in the butter until melted, then add the crushed pretzels and pour over the top of the pretzel crust. Leave to cool at room temperature then transfer to the fridge to chill.

Melt the chocolate in a heatproof bowl over a pan of simmering water (or in the microwave in short bursts) then spread over the top of the set filling mixture. Position the whole pretzels in a circle around the edge of the pie while the chocolate's still soft, then place in the fridge to set. Remove from the fridge 30 minutes before serving.

Serves 12

For the crust:
50g salted pretzels
30g soft dark brown sugar
30g plain flour
65g butter, chilled and diced
1–2 teaspoons milk

For the filling:
100g crunchy peanut butter
75g soft dark brown sugar
200g condensed milk
Generous pinch of salt
40g butter
25g salted pretzels, lightly
  crushed

To top:
150g dark chocolate,
  in chunks
8–12 whole salted pretzels

20cm pie dish or cake tin

STICKY WALNUT CINNAMON SWIRLS

These sticky swirls of buttery dough are packed with toffee-sweet cinnamon walnuts and topped with rich cream cheese frosting. They also work well with a scattering of fresh rosemary needles in the filling, giving them an aromatic, woody depth that sits perfectly alongside the earthy walnut.

Stir together the flour, yeast and salt in a large bowl. Heat the milk until barely tepid, then add to the flour along with the softened butter. Work the ingredients to a rough dough with your hands. Leave the dough to rest, covered, in its bowl for 20 minutes then tip it out onto a clean work surface and knead for 10 minutes, until smoother, more elastic and less sticky. Return to the bowl, cover loosely with cling film and leave to rise at room temperature for 1–2 hours, waiting patiently until it has almost doubled in size.

Beat together the sugar, butter and cinnamon for the filling. Roll the risen dough out on a lightly floured surface until it's roughly 25x50cm, putting your strength into rolling it reasonably thinly and evenly. Spread the butter mixture lightly over the surface of the dough then scatter over the chopped walnuts. Roll the dough up from long edge to long edge to give a 50cm roll.

Trim the tapered ends off then cut the roll into 12 pieces. Arrange the swirls in a greased 20x30cm roasting tin or oven dish, leaving at least a couple of centimetres between them, then drape with cling film and leave to rise for an hour, until visibly puffier and around one and a half times their original size. Preheat the oven to 180°C/fan 160°C/gas mark 4.

Bake the risen buns for 30 minutes, until sizzling, caramelised and golden, then leave to cool in their tin.

To ice the cooled buns, beat the butter, icing sugar and orange zest together until smooth, then stir in the cream cheese a little at a time. Smooth the icing over the top of the buns, letting it sink unevenly into the swirls.

Makes 12

For the dough:
500g strong white flour
10g instant dried yeast
1 teaspoon salt
320ml milk
50g butter, softened

For the filling:
75g soft light brown sugar
75g butter, softened
1 teaspoon ground cinnamon
200g walnuts, coarsely
  chopped

For the icing:
50g butter, softened
75g icing sugar
Zest of ½ orange
175g full-fat cream cheese

HOMEMADE NUT BUTTER

Don't even try to make this nut butter unless you've got a sturdy, powerful food processor at home – you'll need to blitz the nuts on high speed for a fair while to persuade them to release their natural oils and transform from gritty meal to smooth butter. I find the flavour of hazelnuts gives the best results, but almonds or cashews (or even a blend of all three) are also good options.

Preheat the oven to 180°C/fan 160°C/gas mark 4. Spread the hazelnuts over a large baking tray and roast them in the oven for 8–12 minutes, or until they're beginning to darken to a golden brown colour and lose their milky paleness. Take care not to let them brown, as they'll turn bitter. Leave to cool completely.

Transfer the toasted, cooled nuts to a food processor and pulse on low speed until they're coarsely ground. Now turn up the power and blitz on full speed, occasionally pausing to push the mixture back down the sides of the food processor bowl, for 8–10 minutes. It's important not to rush this: keep going until the mixture is very oily and slack. If it's thick and paste-like, it needs longer. The consistency is perfect when it's looser than peanut butter, more viscous than jam. You can add a drop of oil to speed things along if that helps. Once the nut butter is blended, mix in a couple of generous pinches of salt.

You can store this is a sterilised jar for a few days in a cool, dry place, but it's best when fresh. Make it in small batches as and when you need it, and serve on toasted bagels with a thick layer of blueberry jam.

Makes 200g

200g blanched hazelnuts, almonds or cashews

Dash of vegetable, nut or corn oil (optional)

Salt, to taste

SPICED ALMOND AND LAMB FLATBREADS

These flatbreads are loosely based on the Turkish *gözleme* so bountiful in the corner of North London where I used to live: dough rolled to tissue-thin rounds, stuffed with meat, potato or spinach, and cooked on a hotplate until steaming and golden.

Combine the flour, baking powder and salt in a large bowl. Whisk the oil and water together then pour this into the dry ingredients. Work the ingredients roughly together using a spoon before using your hands to bring everything into a smooth dough. Knead it lightly for a couple of minutes before wrapping in cling film and placing in the fridge to rest for an hour or so.

While the dough rests, prepare the filling. Heat the oil in a large frying pan and gently fry the onion over a medium-low heat for 10 minutes, until softened and translucent. Add the garlic and flaked almonds and cook for a minute or so, lightly toasting the nuts. Increase the heat slightly and add the lamb and spices. Cook for 4–5 minutes, stirring regularly, until the lamb is browned all over. Add the sultanas and parsley, season well and leave to cool.

Divide the rested dough into six equal pieces. Roll each piece, on a floured surface, to a circle 20–25cm in diameter. Roll as thinly as you can: the dough should be almost translucent. Spread a sixth of the filling mixture over one half of the circle, leaving a border of a centimetre around the edges. Fold the other half of the circle over the top and pinch the edges together to seal. Dust with a little more flour and roll again until the bread's about one and a half times its original folded size. It doesn't matter if a little of the filling bursts out.

If you're speedy with the filling and rolling of the flatbreads, you can make each one while the previous one is frying. If you're not as confident, just prepare them all and stack them with a square of greaseproof paper between each flatbread, until the whole batch is made and you're ready to start frying.

To cook the flatbreads, heat a glug of oil in a large frying pan and fry the bread for 1 ½–2 minutes on each side over a medium heat. Enjoy while hot.

Makes 6 large flatbreads

For the dough:
400g plain flour
2 teaspoons baking powder
¼ teaspoon salt
90ml olive oil
150ml water

For the filling:
2–3 tablespoons olive oil
1 medium onion, finely chopped
2 large cloves garlic, thinly sliced
50g flaked almonds
375g lamb mince
2 teaspoons ground cumin
2 teaspoons ground coriander
2 teaspoons curry powder
50g sultanas
Small bunch of parsley, finely chopped
Salt and black pepper, to taste
Oil, for frying

CHOCOLATE

SPICED HOT CHOCOLATE

CHOCOLATE RICE KRISPIE CAKES

SALTED CHOCOLATE HONEY SAUCE

5 WAYS WITH CHOCOLATE
CHIP COOKIES

EASY CHOCOLATE BIRTHDAY CAKE

BEJEWELLED CHOCOLATE TILES

Chocolate is as crucial for good health as fruit, lentils, fish and veg – this is one of my most dearly held beliefs. What other food so reliably cheers you, feeds your spirit as well as your stomach, luxuriantly pads out your belly and thighs? I can't think of any other treat that comes in so many shades of garishly glistening wrapper, in so many shapes and sizes and novelty guises. No other ingredient has such a hold over our cravings; no sweet has such cultural currency. Nothing else is sold and bought and guzzled in such exuberant excess. Nourish your soul with it.

SPICED HOT CHOCOLATE

Of course you can multiply the amount below if you want to make a larger batch for several people, but I've given quantities for only one serving. I believe in the restorative powers of hot chocolate: not only the drinking, but also the catharsis of making something so committedly indulgent for you and only you. Let this be your treat to yourself today.

With so few component parts, real hot chocolate stands or falls on the calibre of the ingredients you put in it. Use a reasonably high cocoa percentage chocolate (roughly 70% is fine – no need to buy the wincingly bitter 95% stuff) and, please, full-fat milk.

Warm the milk over a low heat with the sugar, cinnamon, chilli powder and salt until it's scalding hot. Finely chop the chocolate and set it in a mixing bowl. Pour the hot milk over the chocolate chunks, stir in the vanilla and leave to melt for a moment. Stir until the chocolate's smoothly combined with the milk, then decant back into the milk pan and heat very gently until it's piping hot – don't let it boil.

Drink straight away with as many or as few extras – think whipped cream, marshmallows, edible shimmer powder, chocolate shavings – as you want.

Serves 1

250ml full-fat milk

2 teaspoons caster sugar

Couple of pinches of ground cinnamon

Pinch of chilli powder

Pinch of salt

35g dark chocolate

½ teaspoon vanilla extract

CHOCOLATE RICE KRISPIE CAKES

Anyone who raises an eyebrow at the inclusion of this recipe will be missing out. These are one of my favourite un-guilty pleasures. There are times when we all need to throw decorum and good taste to the wind and cook what we want, when we want it. Whether that means cooking spaghetti hoops in the microwave at midnight, serving gummy worms for dessert or, indeed, making Rice Krispie cakes as your big baking project – well that's exactly what you should do.

Line the moulds in the tin with paper cases.

Melt the chocolate, butter and syrup together in a heatproof bowl, either in the microwave or perched over a pan of simmering water. Stir in the puffed rice until it's coated all over with the chocolate mixture, then divide between the paper cases.

I usually have no time or willpower for delayed gratification, but these really do need to be chilled thoroughly before serving. If rushed, they soggily fall apart. Leave them to set in the fridge for at least an hour before enjoying.

Makes 12

150g dark chocolate, finely chopped

75g salted butter, cubed

2 tablespoons golden syrup

75g Rice Krispies

12-hole muffin or cupcake tin

SALTED CHOCOLATE HONEY SAUCE

Whether you're eating it straight from the tub in bed with Netflix or dishing it up in elegant sundae glasses, here's a sauce to perk up even the most basic ice cream. After we'd shot the photos of this sauce, we even greedily dipped long crescents of ripe mango into it as a chocolate fondue. It's best to make this as you need it, in small batches, as the sauce firms and sets as it cools.

Heat the cream in a small pan until it's about to boil, then remove from the heat, add the finely chopped chocolate and stir until smooth. Immediately mix in the butter, honey and salt, adding an extra tablespoon or two of honey if you want the sauce slightly thinner. Keep warm in a water bath until ready to use to ensure the sauce stays silky and pourable.

Makes 250ml, serving 6

150ml double cream

120g dark chocolate, 70% cocoa solids, very finely chopped

30g unsalted butter, softened

4 tablespoons runny honey

¼ teaspoon salt, or to taste

5 WAYS WITH CHOCOLATE CHIP COOKIES

There's no right way to make a chocolate chip cookie: they can be chewy or crunchy, freckled with cocoa nibs or strewn with weighty milk chocolate chunks, cast in a cocoa-y cookie dough or a simple vanilla crumb. With that in mind, the five recipes that follow are to be taken as a rough guide – a few tentative flavour suggestions, from which you can deviate as much or as little as you please. As long as you keep the basic proportions of flour, butter and sugar the same, and stay true to the indulgent spirit of these cookies (no diet versions, please), you can't go far wrong.

AFTER-SCHOOL CHOCOLATE CHUNK COOKIES

This is a really basic chocolate chunk cookie recipe: a mixture of milk and dark chocolate studded through a chewy brown sugar cookie. It's a one-bowl recipe so simple that you can whip up a batch in barely half an hour whenever you feel like treating yourself or the people around you. It's also the base recipe for the four other cookie recipes that follow.

Preheat the oven to 180°C/fan 160°C/gas mark 4 and line a couple of large baking trays with baking parchment.

Beat the butter and sugar together in a large bowl until smooth then add the egg, vanilla, flour, bicarbonate of soda, salt and the chocolate chunks. Combine thoroughly, but don't over-mix.

Spoon mounds of the cookie dough onto the prepared trays, leaving plenty of space between them. Bake for 12–14 minutes until the cookies are golden brown and well spread and the chocolate chunks molten and gooey. They'll be really soft at this point but will firm up as they cool, so leave them undisturbed on their baking trays until they're more or less cooled.

Makes 10–12 cookies

125g salted butter, well softened

150g soft light brown sugar

1 large egg, lightly beaten

1 teaspoon vanilla extract

200g plain flour

½ teaspoon bicarbonate of soda

Good pinch of salt

75g milk chocolate, in chunks

75g dark chocolate, in small chunks

triple chocolate
midnight cookies

5 ways with
chocolate chip
cookies

after school
chocolate
chunk
cookies

chocolate
l cookies

olive oil chocolate
chip cookies

tter
brown sugar

vs chunks

(160°)

14 minutes

OLIVE OIL CHOCOLATE CHIP COOKIES

Follow the recipe on page 315, but swap the butter for 100ml extra-virgin olive oil, and use all dark chocolate in place of the milk and dark mixture. You need a good-quality, high cocoa percentage chocolate that'll be able to stand its ground against the fruity clout of the oil. Sprinkle a few sea salt flakes on top too if you want.

WHITE CHOCOLATE PRETZEL COOKIES

Follow the recipe on page 315, but use 150g white chocolate for the chocolate chunks, and add 50g lightly crushed crunchy salted pretzels to the dough, too. The salty tang of the pretzels really offsets the sickly sweetness of the white chocolate.

ESPRESSO RYE COOKIES

Here's a cookie worth waking up for in the morning. Get a dose of caffeine and the virtuousness of a little wholemeal all in one. Follow the recipe on page 315, but replace half of the plain flour with dark rye flour, add 2 tablespoons of ground coffee (not instant granules) and be sure to use all dark chocolate. Bake for slightly longer than specified in the recipe: give the cookies 15–17 minutes in total.

TRIPLE CHOCOLATE COOKIES

This is the kind of dark, chocolatey cookie I want when midnight hunger sends me rummaging through the kitchen for my sweet fix. Use 175g plain flour in place of the 200g specified on page 315, and add 30g cocoa powder with it. Stir through 150g of a mixture of white and milk chocolate chunks once the cookie dough is ready, then portion and bake as instructed.

EASY CHOCOLATE BIRTHDAY CAKE

This is the cake I make for birthdays, celebrations and special occasions when I just need a no-fuss recipe. There's no compromise on flavour, though: light brown sugar adds a toffee sweetness, vanilla sits in harmony with the cocoa, coffee lends a welcome darkness while the saltiness of the butter brings the whole thing into focus. It's got all the depth of the richest chocolate cakes, but with the lightness of a Victoria sponge.

If you want something a little more grown up, ice the cake as detailed below, chill it well then glaze with a thin coat of ganache.

Preheat the oven to 180°C/fan 160°C/gas mark 4. Grease the cake tins and line their bases with circles of baking parchment.

Beat the butter with the sugar in a large mixing bowl for several minutes, until perfectly smooth and light. Stir in the cocoa powder and vanilla extract. Add the eggs one at a time, beating well between each to minimise clumping and curdling. Stir the flour and baking powder together in a separate bowl then add this mixture to the wet ingredients, mixing until smooth. Add the coffee and fold in to give a soft, velvety batter.

Divide the batter between the two prepared tins and bake for 30–35 minutes, until well risen and springy to touch. A small knife inserted into the centre of each cake should emerge with no more than a couple of crumbs stuck to it. Leave the cakes to cool completely in their tins before unmoulding.

For the buttercream, beat the butter until smooth then stir in the cocoa powder and vanilla extract. Sift in the icing sugar a third at a time, mixing well as you go. Finally, stir in the coffee. The buttercream should be luxuriantly thick, but soft enough to spread on the cakes without ripping them. Add a dash of extra milk or coffee to slacken if necessary.

Smooth a thick layer of buttercream over one of the cake layers then sandwich with the second layer and ice the top. Spread the remaining buttercream generously around the sides of the cake. Decorate with as much sparkle as you like.

For the cake:

275g salted butter, very soft

275g soft light brown sugar

75g cocoa powder

2½ teaspoons vanilla extract

4 large eggs

225g plain flour

3 teaspoons baking powder

150ml weak black coffee, cooled (or 150ml milk)

For the buttercream:

225g salted butter, softened

50g cocoa powder

2 teaspoons vanilla extract

325g icing sugar

2 teaspoons instant coffee dissolved in 2 teaspoons water

Two 20cm round cake tins, preferably loose-bottomed or spring-form

BEJEWELLED CHOCOLATE TILES

When it comes to last-minute presents, there's a better way than crumpled boxes of Quality Street and bottles of corner-shop fizz. These chocolate tiles are what I make when I need a birthday gift or dinner party offering, but have only an hour before I need to scramble out of the house. Because you can add any toppings you please, these can be as delicate or extravagant, as cluttered or tastefully subdued as you like, just try to keep the colours and textures varied. Here are a few toppings that you could use, though the list is by no means exhaustive: poppy seeds, sesame seeds, candied rose petals, pistachios, glacé cherries, candied ginger, roasted hazelnuts, chopped dried apricots, sultanas, dried Morello cherries, chopped candied peel, crystallised violet, freeze-dried strawberry or raspberry pieces and blanched almonds.

Break the chocolate into small chunks and melt in a bowl set over a pan of barely simmering water. You can melt chocolate in the microwave too, but you'll need to take care and stir regularly – perhaps every 15–20 seconds – otherwise the chocolate will burn and become grainy. Lay a sheet of baking parchment over a tray, and pour the melted chocolate on, letting it spread to a 15cm circle (you can guide it into a neater, rectangular shape if you prefer). Scatter on the toppings. Leave the chocolate to cool and set before wrapping in greaseproof paper or cellophane.

Makes 1

100g dark or white chocolate

60g dried fruit, nuts, crystallised flowers and seeds

More recipes with chocolate:
Spelt Pear Chocolate Crumble, page 117
White Chocolate and Passion Fruit Pots, page 135
Warming Chocolate Chip Jaffa Pudding, page 144
Salted Milk Chocolate Blackberry Mousse Cake, page 169
Intense Chocolate and Cardamom Ice Cream, page 213
Pretzel Peanut Butter Pie, page 303
Black Sesame and Green Tea 'Oreos', page 342
Sticky Midnight Gingerbread, page 346
Chocolate Stout Pudding, page 357

SUGAR

MALTED CHOCOLATE LAYER CAKE

BLACK TREACLE COCOA BROWNIES
WITH CLOTTED CREAM

SHINE THEORY CAKE TRUFFLES

HONEY BUNDT CAKE

TOFFEE MUSCOVADO TART

BLUEBERRY YOGHURT LOAF CAKE

HONEYCOMB

Sweetness has always been my weakness. The recipes in this section run with that – no clever tricks, no slipping sweet into savoury or savoury into sweet, just unapologetically sugary bliss in shades of cake, brownie, tart and candy. More often than not it's white sugar (usually caster, whose fine granules dissolve more readily than the coarser granulated sugar) that we use in cakes and biscuits, but be resourceful and you can swap in other sugars and syrups – ones that contribute caramel notes or bitter streaks, fragrance or even malty depth and not simply sweetness. I've tried to use a good variety throughout this section, including honey, black treacle, muscovado and malt alongside the usual suspects.

MALTED CHOCOLATE LAYER CAKE

There's a double hit of malt in this sweetly chocolatey layer cake – first from the malt extract folded into the cake batter and through the buttercream, and then from the Maltesers crushed and strewn between the layers. You can find malt extract in any high street health food shop, and in a few of the larger supermarkets, too: it's sold in jars, has a rich brown colour and a consistency somewhere between the sticky thickness of honey and black treacle.

Preheat the oven to 180°C/fan 160°C/gas mark 4. Grease the cake tins and line their bases with baking parchment.

Beat the butter and brown sugar together for a good 2–3 minutes, until smooth and light. Stir in the malt extract and vanilla, then add the eggs one at a time, whisking well between each one. Don't worry if the mixture's a little curdled at this point – it'll come together smoothly as soon as the dry ingredients go in.

Mix the flour and baking powder together in a separate bowl before adding to the wet mixture. Beat briefly to combine and give a smooth, loose batter. Divide the batter between the two prepared cake tins and bake for 25–35 minutes, or until the cakes are well risen and golden brown. A small knife inserted into the centre of each cake should emerge with no more than a crumb or two stuck to it. Leave the cakes to cool for 10 minutes in their tins before unmoulding them and transferring to wire racks to cool completely.

Once the cakes are completely cool (and you really do need to be patient here, because if cut while warm they'll crumble), slice each layer horizontally in half with a large, serrated knife to give a total of four thin layers.

For the buttercream, beat together the butter, cocoa powder, malt extract and vanilla until smooth. Add the icing sugar a little at a time (add it all at once and it'll take forever to work the ingredients together) and mix until the buttercream is thick and well combined. Add enough milk to loosen the buttercream to a light, spreadable consistency – it ought to be soft enough to spread over the delicate cake layers without ripping them.

Serves 10

For the cake:
250g salted butter, softened
200g soft light brown sugar
125g malt extract
2 teaspoons vanilla extract
4 large eggs
300g plain flour
3 teaspoons baking powder

For the buttercream:
250g salted butter, softened
40g cocoa powder
3 tablespoons malt extract
2 teaspoons vanilla extract
350g icing sugar
1–2 tablespoons milk
150–250g Maltesers

Two 20cm round cake tins, preferably loose-bottomed or spring-form

Spread a fifth of the buttercream over each of the four cake layers. Sandwich the sponges together, sprinkling a few crushed Maltesers between the layers. When it's assembled, spread the remaining buttercream around the sides of the cake in a thin layer. Decorate the top of the cake with crushed or whole Maltesers however you want.

BLACK TREACLE COCOA BROWNIES WITH CLOTTED CREAM

The best brownies I've ever made: dense and fudgy, the depth of the cocoa echoed with bitter black treacle, the kind of brownie that's so rich you need to eat it in moderation... two, three, four, five times a day.

Preheat the oven to 180°C/fan 160°C/gas mark 4 and line the tin with baking parchment. (Any similar-sized tin will do – a 20cm round cake tin will be more or less equivalent in volume, while a 20cm square tin will give you a slightly shallower brownie, so decrease the baking time accordingly.)

Melt the butter and treacle together in a pan over a low heat then set aside to cool a little. Whisk the sugar and eggs in a large bowl for 2–3 minutes, until very smooth and slightly bubbly. Stir the flour, cocoa powder and salt together in a separate bowl, breaking up any rogue clumps as you go. Add the melted butter to the egg and sugar mixture, then the dry ingredients mix. Beat until smooth and glossy.

Spoon the brownie batter into the prepared tin and lightly smooth the surface. Bake for 25–30 minutes. For a perfectly dense, fudgy texture, cook only until the brownie no longer jiggles in the centre when you gently shake the tin. The surface should be dried and even, and a knife inserted into the centre should come out with just a little stickiness on it – don't wait until the knife emerges totally clean, or you'll have cooked it too long.

Leave the brownie to cool and set completely in its tin before cutting into portions and serving with scoops of thick clotted cream.

Makes 9

150g unsalted butter

3 tablespoons black treacle

200g soft light brown sugar

2 large eggs

90g plain flour

75g cocoa powder

¼ teaspoon salt

150g clotted cream, to serve

15x22cm rectangular cake tin

SHINE THEORY CAKE TRUFFLES

Shine Theory is the idea that if you help the people around you to grow, you'll shine brighter for it. It's the opposite of those self-serving philosophies that make rivals of teammates and enemies of friends. It's about nurturing the success of others, and being nurtured in turn, rather than falling back on an every-woman-for-herself individualism. Shine Theory was born of a certain brand of ebullient Tumblr feminism, all slogans and cute graphics – the enthusiastic spirit of it might delight or confound you, but either way the message is still one to hold to. These cake truffles (made with cake crumbs and chocolate in place of the usual truffle ganache) are shimmering reminders of your new life motto: share them with your friends and friends-to-be.

Preheat the oven to 180°C/fan 160°C/gas mark 4. Grease the tin and line the base with a circle of baking parchment.

Cream the butter and sugar together until light and fluffy then stir in the vanilla extract and cocoa powder. Add the egg and milk and beat to combine. Measure in the flour and baking powder, stirring everything gently together until you're left with a smooth batter. Spoon the batter into the prepared cake tin and bake for around 20 minutes, until the cake is well risen, golden brown and cooked through to its centre. Leave to cool for a few minutes in its tin before unmoulding and letting it cool completely.

Once the cake is at room temperature, blitz it in the food processor until it's reduced to fine crumbs. If you want to do this by hand, just break it up and rub it between your fingertips. If your oven runs a little hot, the sides of your cake might be quite dry and browned – if so, trim these edges off before you crumb the cake.

Melt the 150g dark chocolate in a heatproof bowl, either in the microwave or set over a pan of gently simmering water. In a large bowl, add the melted chocolate to the crumbed cake mixture along with the milk. Work everything together using your hands. The mixture needs to be just sticky enough to hold in balls when you squeeze it together. If it's too dry, add a splash of extra milk; if it's too sticky, put it in the fridge for a little while to firm up.

Makes 24

For the cake crumbs:
100g salted butter, softened
100g caster sugar
2 teaspoons vanilla extract
2 tablespoons cocoa powder
1 large egg
2 tablespoons milk
100g plain flour
1 teaspoon baking powder

To assemble the truffles:
150g dark chocolate
1–2 tablespoons milk
250g dark or white chocolate
Edible lustre powder

20cm round cake tin, preferably loose-bottomed or spring-form

Roll the cake mix into 24 small balls and arrange on a tray. Place in the fridge for an hour to chill and firm. Once the cake truffles have chilled, melt the 250g white or dark chocolate and dip the truffles in it until coated in a light, even layer. Set back on the tray and return to the fridge for the chocolate coating to firm.

Once the chocolate is set, dust the shimmer powder liberally over the truffles, using a make-up brush or small paintbrush to apply a light layer. The truffles will keep in the fridge for a couple of days.

HONEY BUNDT CAKE

I love the simplicity of this honey cake. It's best to use a good, flavourful honey if you can afford it (I like orange blossom), but thanks to the accompanying accents of orange zest, cinnamon, warm ginger and dark brown sugar here, the quality of the honey isn't make or break, so don't worry too much about getting the top-of-the-line stuff.

Though I make this in a Bundt tin, the batter only half fills the tin, making a smaller, more manageable cake, and one less likely to overcook at its edges. You can double the quantities though if you want a full-size Bundt cake, or for a more modest version make the amount instructed below and bake in a 900g loaf tin.

Preheat the oven to 180°C/fan 160°C/gas mark 4. Grease the tin with a little butter or margarine (this cake is prone to sticking on every curve and crease, so do be thorough), then toss a tablespoon of flour in to stick to the fat and coat it in a very thin, even layer.

Whisk together the oil, honey, brown sugar, vanilla extract and orange zest, then beat in the eggs. Add the dry ingredients and stir to get a smooth, loose batter. Pour the batter into the prepared tin and bake for 30–35 minutes, or until a small knife pushed into the deepest part of the cake comes out clean. If you're baking a double quantity or cooking this in a 900g loaf tin, you'll need to bake for at least 45 minutes, checking at regular intervals thereafter until it's done.

Let the cake cool completely in its tin before unmoulding it. You could make a runny drizzle icing using water, vanilla extract and icing sugar if you want, but I think the cake works perfectly well with just a snowy dusting of icing sugar.

Serves 8

75ml vegetable oil

175g runny honey

75g soft dark brown sugar

1½ teaspoons vanilla extract

Zest of 1 orange

3 medium or large eggs

150g plain flour, plus extra
 for the tin

100g ground almonds

2 teaspoons baking powder

½ teaspoon ground cinnamon

½ teaspoon ground ginger

¼ teaspoon salt

Icing sugar, to dust

Bundt tin or 900g loaf tin

TOFFEE MUSCOVADO TART

This tart is inspired by the muscovado tart at Murano in London, which I've heard so much about but never had the luxury of tasting. This version, then, is born from a daydream – something deliciously real pulled from the wistful imaginings of my stomach and my mind. Because my vision of this tart was so blurred around the edges, I had the freedom to make it as sweet or as sophisticated, as dark or as mellow as I pleased. I opted for something comfortably in the middle on all spectrums: a tender shortcrust pastry around an orange-scented caramel filling, heavy with cream and condensed milk.

To make the pastry, rub together the flour and butter until you've got a fine-textured, crumbly mixture. Add the milk and cut it into the dry mixture until the pastry starts to hold together in small clumps. If there's a lot of dry flour left, add a splash more milk. Press the dough into a round, wrap in cling film and refrigerate for 30 minutes or so, or until it's less sticky and easier to roll out.

Roll out the pastry on a floured work surface until it's big enough to line the tin, and is no more than 5mm thick. Gently transfer the pastry to the tin, using the rolling pin to help you guide it over, and press firmly into the sides. Place in the fridge to chill for 30 minutes while you preheat the oven to 180°C/fan 160°C/ gas mark 4.

Once the pastry case is chilled, prick the base all over with a fork, line with baking parchment and fill with baking weights (uncooked rice or lentils work well if you don't have ceramic baking beans). Bake for 20 minutes like this before removing the parcel of baking parchment and weights and cooking for a further 3–5 minutes, uncovered.

While the pastry cooks, prepare the filling by stirring together all the ingredients. As soon as the pastry case is ready, turn down the oven to 150°C/fan 130°C/gas mark 2.

Pour the filling into the pastry and bake for 45–55 minutes, or until the tart is set, all but for a slight wobble at its centre. Leave to cool completely to room temperature before moving to the fridge to chill. Serve with whipped cream, sweetened with a little sugar and spiked with Cointreau.

Serves 12

For the pastry:

175g plain flour

100g butter, firm but not fridge-cold, cubed

2 tablespoons milk

(or 300g ready-made shortcrust pastry)

For the filling:

400ml condensed milk

150ml double cream

75g dark muscovado sugar

5 medium or large egg yolks

1 teaspoon vanilla extract

Zest of ½ orange

¼ teaspoon salt

23cm round flan or tart tin

BLUEBERRY YOGHURT LOAF CAKE

This is one of my favourite cakes for lazy days, when strenuous whisking, creaming and mixing are not on the cards. Here you just stir the ingredients together, spoon the batter into the tin and, just under an hour later, remove the light, blueberry-studded cake from the oven.

I use almond oil in this cake because its mellow nuttiness is a good partner for the blueberries and lemon, but you can use cheaper sunflower oil if that's what you've got in the cupboard. Mix in a little extra vanilla extract if so, or even a splash of almond extract, to add depth.

Preheat the oven to 180°C/fan 160°C/gas mark 4 and line the tin with baking parchment.

In a large bowl, whisk together the almond oil, yoghurt, sugar, eggs, vanilla extract and lemon zest. In a separate bowl, stir together the flour, baking powder and salt. Pour the dry ingredients into the yoghurt mixture along with the blueberries and fold the lot very gently together, taking care not to mix any more than is necessary: over-zealous stirring at this stage could result in a tough cake later.

Pour the batter into the prepared loaf tin and bake for 50-55 minutes, or until a small knife inserted into the middle comes out basically clean. Leave to cool for 15 minutes in its tin before unmoulding and setting on a wire rack to cool completely.

Makes 1 loaf cake, serving 6
100ml almond oil
125g full-fat natural yoghurt
175g caster sugar
2 large eggs
1 teaspoon vanilla extract
Zest of 2 lemons
225g plain flour
1½ teaspoons baking powder
Pinch of salt
150–200g blueberries

900g loaf tin

HONEYCOMB

Working with hot sugar terrifies me, but my candy cravings trump my worry. If someone as nervous as I am can make honeycomb, so can you – just make sure you use a large enough pan, keep a constant eye on the boiling syrup and have the bicarb measured and ready to be poured into the caramel as soon as it's up to temperature. A sugar thermometer is really useful here, but it's not essential; if you don't have one, let droplets of the caramel fall into a glass of fridge-cold water at intervals through the cooking: at first the caramel will set loose and stringy, then it'll clump into fudgy lumps and then – when it's ready – it'll solidify into rock-hard balls when it hits the water.

Line the cake tin (a bigger roasting dish will work, though the honeycomb pieces will be slightly shallower) with baking parchment and grease the paper generously with vegetable oil. Measure the sugar and golden syrup into a small pan with a splash of water. Hook a sugar thermometer, if you have one, onto the side of the pan and set over a medium-low heat. Stir gently until the sugar has nearly dissolved, then stop stirring, increase to a medium-high heat and leave to bubble, untouched, until the sugar thermometer reads 145–150°C (this may be labelled 'hard crack' stage on your thermometer). The closer you let the reading creep to 150°C, the more brittle and less chewy your honeycomb will be.

As soon as the mixture is up to the desired temperature, add the bicarbonate of soda and immediately whisk in using a large wire whisk, taking care not to burn yourself on the hot caramel as it foams up. Pour the honeycomb mixture into the prepared baking tin or dish straight away and leave to cool to room temperature. Once it's completely cool, smash or cut the honeycomb into jagged shards.

Makes a 20cm square slab of honeycomb

Vegetable oil, for greasing

125g caster sugar

75g golden syrup

1 teaspoon bicarbonate of soda

20cm square cake tin

TEA AND COFFEE

CHEWY EARL GREY SANDWICH BISCUITS

BLACK SESAME AND GREEN TEA 'OREOS'

COFFEE BOURBON GLAZED RIBS

COFFEE CREAM MERINGUE
WITH CHERRIES

STICKY MIDNIGHT GINGERBREAD

AFFOGATO

We drink a lot of tea and coffee here in the UK, but we're less inventive when it comes to using them in our cooking. It seems a terrible waste: if something can taste so good just spooned carelessly into a cup and stirred with boiling water, imagine how spectacular it could be when prepared with a little more care. You could mix matcha green tea powder with butter and sugar, for example, for a vivid green buttercream, or perhaps beat trusty Earl Grey into chewy cookies, or pair black tea with treacle and hot ginger spice. There are even ways to work tea and coffee into savoury dishes, as in the coffee-spiked ribs on page 343. The recipes in this section are just a few ideas to get you started and to move beyond the go-to coffee and walnut cake, but you should play around with different teas and coffees (and even hot malt drinks, herbal teas and spice blends) as you get more confident.

CHEWY EARL GREY SANDWICH BISCUITS

Aromatic Earl Grey sits well alongside citrus flavours in these cute sandwich biscuits. If tea's not your bag, plain orange peel cookies would work fine, though I'd be tempted to take the edge off the sweetness with a little chopped pistachio in the dough.

Preheat the oven to 180°C/fan 160°C/gas mark 4 and line a couple of baking trays with baking parchment.

Beat the butter with the sugar until perfectly smooth and light before stirring in the egg yolks. In a separate bowl, mix the flour with the bicarbonate of soda, then tear open the teabags and add the tea. Add this dry mixture to the wet ingredients, mashing together until roughly combined, then work in the chopped candied peel.

Roll teaspoons of the dough into balls, space well apart on the lined baking trays and press each ball down to a round just under 1cm thick. Bake for 10 minutes, then leave to cool completely on the trays.

For the buttercream, beat the butter with the contents of the tea bags, the icing sugar and milk until smooth. Spoon a little onto half of the biscuits, then sandwich with the remaining biscuits. These are best eaten on the day you make them, but if you want to keep them longer store the biscuits and buttercream separately until you're ready to put them together and eat, otherwise the biscuits will grow soggy.

Makes 14–16 sandwich biscuits

100g unsalted butter, softened

125g caster sugar

2 large egg yolks

150g plain flour

½ teaspoon bicarbonate of soda

3 Earl Grey tea bags

50g candied peel, finely chopped

For the buttercream:

100g unsalted butter, softened

2 Earl Grey tea bags

200g icing sugar

2 teaspoons milk

BLACK SESAME AND GREEN TEA 'OREOS'

Ground black sesame seeds add a toasted, nutty flavour and rich colour to these imitation Oreos. Look for black sesame seeds and matcha green tea powder in Japanese food shops or online, but it's no disaster if you can't get hold of either: use white sesame seeds instead (first toasted for 10–15 minutes in a 200°C/fan 180°C/gas mark 6 oven) and swap the green tea powder for vanilla extract. You can grind sencha green tea for a similar effect, too, but the flavour won't be same, the powder won't be smooth and the colour won't be as bright. I find that vanilla is the safer bet if matcha powder isn't an option.

Grind the sesame seeds in a food processor or coffee grinder until they're reduced to a mealy powder, then set aside. Mix the flour and cocoa powder in a large bowl, then rub the butter in, using your fingertips, until no visible flakes of butter remain. The mixture should resemble fine breadcrumbs. Toss through the ground sesame seeds, sugar, baking powder and salt. Add the water and use a small knife to cut the liquid into the mixture until all of the flour has been moistened. Lightly press the mixture together to a flat disc, adding a drop more water if necessary, then wrap tightly in cling film and refrigerate for 15–30 minutes. Preheat the oven to 180°C/fan 160°C/gas mark 4 and line a large baking tray with baking parchment.

Roll out the dough on a floured work surface to around 20x35cm, and 3–5mm thick. Use a 4–5cm round pastry cutter to stamp out circles, and arrange the circles on the prepared tray (line a second tray if they won't comfortably fit on one). Re-roll the offcuts and stamp out more biscuits, if you want. Bake for 12–14 minutes, then leave the biscuits to cool before carefully peeling away from the baking parchment.

For the buttercream, beat the butter with the green tea powder until smooth (and bright green), then gradually stir in the icing sugar. Add a splash of milk if the mixture is too stiff. Place a teaspoonful of the buttercream on each of half of the batch of biscuits, then sandwich with the remaining biscuits, pressing gently down to help squash the buttercream and bring it flush with the edges of the biscuit.

Makes 16–18 biscuit sandwiches

For the biscuits:

75g black sesame seeds

100g plain flour

2 tablespoons cocoa powder

80g butter, firm but not fridge-cold, cubed

50g caster sugar

1 teaspoon baking powder

Pinch of salt

2 teaspoons cold water

For the buttercream:

100g butter, softened

2 teaspoons matcha green tea powder

200g icing sugar

COFFEE BOURBON GLAZED RIBS

These sticky ribs need a long, slow cook but the end result – perfectly juicy, tender, sweet-savoury meat – is well worth the effort. The coffee in the rub and in the glaze lends an aromatic depth that mellows the sauce's sweetness and sits well against the mildness of the meat itself. Feel free to adjust the ratios of the ingredients in the glaze to suit your tastes – some might prefer a spicier version, with extra Tabasco and even a pinch of cayenne, while others might want to play up the glaze's fruitiness with a spoon or two of brown sauce.

Preheat the oven to 160°C/fan 140°C/gas mark 3. Set up a large oven tray or roasting dish with a wire rack or grill tray on it – resting the ribs on this as they cook will help the heat to circulate evenly. If you don't have a rack, just make sure you turn the ribs over halfway through cooking.

Stir together the sugar, coffee, paprika, garlic, cayenne and salt for the rub, and massage into the ribs, gently pressing the spices, sugar and coffee onto the meat. Wrap the ribs loosely in one big parcel of kitchen foil, making sure that the foil is two layers thick, and scrunch the edges together to seal.

Place the foil parcel on the rack or oven tray and bake for 2 hours, until the meat is tender, juicy and shrinking away from the bone. Then leave to rest in the foil for 15 minutes and preheat the grill to high.

While the ribs rest, prepare the coffee bourbon glaze. Combine all of the ingredients from the tomato ketchup through to the Tabasco in a small pan, add the water and set over a low heat. Whisk until smooth then cook until the sauce is glossy, thick and beginning to bubble.

Unwrap the ribs from their foil parcel and brush each generously with the glaze. Set under the grill for 2–3 minutes, until the glaze is bubbling. Serve immediately, decanting any leftover glaze into a small dish as a dipping sauce.

Serves 4

For the rub:

75g soft dark brown sugar

2 tablespoons instant coffee granules

1 tablespoon smoked paprika

2 cloves garlic, crushed

½ teaspoon cayenne pepper

¼ teaspoon salt

1kg pork ribs

For the glaze:

6 tablespoons tomato ketchup

6 tablespoons soft dark brown sugar

3 tablespoons bourbon

2 tablespoons Worcestershire sauce

1 tablespoon smoked paprika

1 tablespoon cornflour

2 teaspoons instant coffee granules

2 cloves garlic, crushed

Dash of Tabasco or other hot sauce, to taste

75ml water

COFFEE CREAM MERINGUE WITH CHERRIES

This is a meringue roulade: a sheet of delicate meringue rolled with a fruit and cream filling. You can make a simple version by cooking little mounds of meringue (check the recipe for Roasted Strawberry Cream Pavlovas on page 167 for method tips) and serving them 'free-form' with dollops of sweet cream and cherries, but I think that much of the appeal of this pretty dessert is the way that the meringue – crisp on top and mousse-soft within – crackles and splinters as you wrap it around the filling. Add a splash of marsala, whisky or brandy to the cream before whisking for a boozy kick.

Preheat the oven to 160°C/fan 140°C/gas mark 3 and line the roasting tin or Swiss roll tin with baking parchment.

In a scrupulously clean, dry glass or metal bowl, whisk the egg whites until they're densely foamy throughout (this could take anywhere between 1 and 3 minutes, depending on the freshness of your eggs and the efficacy of your whisk). Once the eggs are aerated, add the sugar a quarter at a time, whisking on full speed for 30–45 seconds between each addition. Continue whisking until the meringue is very thick and glossy and holds in stiff peaks.

Dissolve the coffee in 4 teaspoons of hot water, let cool and then stir into the meringue, taking care not to overmix. The coffee will deflate the meringue a little and slacken it, but it should still be thick and smooth. Spread over the parchment-lined baking tray and cook in the oven for 45 minutes, or until well risen and crisp on top, but soft within. Leave to cool.

Whisk the double cream and sugar together until thick enough to hold soft peaks. Lay a fresh sheet of baking parchment down on the work surface and carefully tip the cooled meringue upside-down onto it. Peel off the original sheet of baking parchment from the meringue, then spread the double cream all over and scatter over the cherries.

Roll the meringue up from long edge to long edge, using the baking parchment underneath to guide it as you roll, then place in the fridge for at least an hour to settle and for the flavours to blend before serving in thick slices.

Serves 6–8

4 large egg whites

250g caster sugar

4 teaspoons instant coffee granules

300ml double cream

50g caster sugar

175g frozen cherries, defrosted (or 225g fresh cherries, pitted)

20x30cm roasting tin or Swiss roll tin

STICKY MIDNIGHT GINGERBREAD

This is the darkest, dampest gingerbread cake I know: black treacle, tea and cocoa powder each adding depth to the warm ginger sweetness. You could contrast the darkness and stickiness of the cake with a light cream cheese frosting (just a little softened butter mixed with cream cheese and icing sugar to taste) but this version sticks with a traditional dusting of icing sugar for simplicity's sake.

Preheat the oven to 180°C/fan 160°C/gas mark 4. Line the base of the dish or tin with baking parchment and grease the sides with a little butter.

Melt the butter with the treacle in a small pan, decant into a large mixing bowl and stir in the brown sugar and grated ginger. Whisk in the eggs and then the flour, cocoa powder, ground ginger, baking powder and salt. Once the batter is smooth, beat in the tea and immediately pour the mix into the prepared tin. Bake immediately (the batter will deflate if you leave it sitting around before cooking) for 35–45 minutes, until a small knife pushed into the centre of the cake emerges more or less clean.

This is a cake that really benefits from being left to cool and rest. Once it's at room temperature, cover it with cling film and leave for 24–48 hours to mellow, if you can. If waiting that long is out of the question you can of course enjoy this the same day as baking, but it won't have quite the same depth of flavour. When you're ready to eat it, dust liberally with icing sugar before cutting into generous slices.

Serves 12

225g butter

225g black treacle

225g soft dark brown sugar

Thumb-sized piece of fresh ginger, peeled and grated

3 large eggs

375g plain flour

4 tablespoons cocoa powder

2 tablespoons ground ginger

4½ teaspoons baking powder

½ teaspoon salt

375ml strong black tea, still hot

Icing sugar, to dust

20x30cm roasting dish or tin

AFFOGATO

This is simply hot espresso and vanilla ice cream, putting to rest the idea that dessert needs to be complicated to be impressive. Eating this Italian dessert is a disorientating experience, with jarring flavours, textures and temperatures, but these contradictions will dance across your palate with dream-like lightness. Because there are only the two ingredients here, it really does pay to opt for quality when you buy. A dense, vanilla-flecked ice cream will melt more slowly than a cheap soft-scoop one, and it'll be better able to stand up to the bitterness of the coffee, while the espresso should be a full-bodied one, with toasted, chocolate notes.

Scoop the ice cream into four small glasses, bowls or ramekins. The colder and firmer the ice cream, the better. Divide the hot coffee between the servings, pouring it carefully around – rather than directly on top of – the ice cream, to prolong the melting time. Serve immediately.

Serves 4

4 small scoops of vanilla ice cream

150ml strong espresso coffee

More recipes with tea and coffee:
Summer Pineapple Camomile Cake, page 126

BOOZE

STICKY MALT AND ALE LOAF

MAGIC LEMON SHERBET
COCKTAILS

PRETTY IN PINK COCKTAILS

CHOCOLATE STOUT PUDDING

FIGS AND WHITE WINE
MASCARPONE CREAM

Alcohol is expensive, and I used to squirm at the thought of using it in cooking and diluting the very boozy hit that makes it so pricey in the first place. I'd drink even the dregs of lukewarm Strongbow and £2.99 bottles of screw-top rosé, but for some reason I couldn't bring myself to donate a splash of white wine to a risotto or lace a cake batter with a little brown ale. Since learning to cook I've changed my ways, though, and while I'm still mindful of the cost of alcohol, I've let go a little when it comes to using it in my food. The great thing about cooking with alcohol is that all but the very cheapest, sweetest drinks are packed with flavour already – from smooth stout to malty ales, bright white wines, gin and warming whisky – so a little goes a long way. The recipes here are mainly sweet, as it happens, but you can find a lemony risotto with white wine on page 145 and a cider-spiked fish pie on page 274 should you want to broaden your repertoire.

STICKY MALT AND ALE LOAF

There's a malt loaf recipe in my first book, *Crumb*, that sweetens the hit of malt with dates. This version has evolved and grown up, using brown ale in place of the fruit for an extra layer of smooth, malty flavour. Whether you serve this toasted or untoasted, spreading this teatime loaf with plenty of salted butter is non-negotiable.

Preheat the oven to 180°C/fan 160°C/gas mark 4, and grease and line the tin. Melt the butter over a low heat, then whisk in the brown ale and malt extract. Remove from the heat, stir in the sugar and add the eggs one at a time.

Mix the flour, baking powder and salt in a separate bowl, then pour into the wet ingredients and stir lightly to combine. Pour the batter into the prepared loaf tin and bake for around 1 hour, or until a knife inserted into the centre comes out with only a crumb or two stuck to it. Leave to cool completely in its tin before unmoulding and serving.

Serves 6–8

50g unsalted butter
125ml brown ale
150g malt extract
125g soft dark brown sugar
2 large eggs, lightly beaten
250g plain flour
2 teaspoons baking powder
¼ teaspoon salt

900g loaf tin

MAGIC LEMON SHERBET COCKTAILS

My most vivid memories from the *Harry Potter* books are the feasts, treats and sweets: scenes in the Great Hall where food is magicked onto plates from thin air; the train snack trolley, where Harry swaps a fistful of heavy coins for everything from pumpkin pasties to chocolate frogs; tankards of thick butterbeer. I pored over these indulgent descriptions for so long that my mouth would water, and real meals suddenly seemed disappointingly dull. There were a few foods that translated seamlessly between book and real life though, and sherbet lemons were one of them: Albus Dumbledore's favourite muggle sweet became my treat and my link to that wizarding world. Here's a cocktail in homage to sherbet lemons: fizzing as tartly, as sweetly and as exuberantly as eccentric Dumbledore himself.

Mash the sorbet in a measuring jug or cocktail shaker until it's smooth and thickly slushy. Gradually whisk in the orange juice followed by the vodka and lemon juice.

Cut a lemon wedge from the other half of the lemon and run this around the rims of two glasses (if you have them, Martini glasses look great). Tip the sherbet onto a plate and dip the rims of the glasses into it to coat the edge with a little fizzy sherbet. Divide the cocktail between the two glasses and serve each with a strip of lemon zest.

Serves 2

100g lemon sorbet, slightly softened

75ml orange juice

50ml vodka

Juice of ½ lemon

1 pack sherbet Dip Dabs

2 wide strips lemon zest

PRETTY IN PINK COCKTAILS

These grapefruit gin cocktails blush the most beautiful pink. It's a colour very similar to Andie's trademark rose hues in *Pretty in Pink*, perhaps my favourite teen movie, with an aesthetic that is cutesy, preppy, camp, trashy and sweet all at once.

Pour the grapefruit juice, gin and orange juice into a cocktail shaker or jug. Whisk the grenadine with the honey until smooth, then add to the juice mixture along with the mint leaves. Strain into four ice-filled glasses and top up with a little soda water.

Makes 4

200ml red grapefruit juice
  (from 2–3 grapefruits)

200ml gin

100ml orange juice

50ml grenadine

4 teaspoons honey

12 mint leaves, bruised

Soda water

CHOCOLATE STOUT PUDDING

The post-Christmas lull is a difficult time of year, hovering between the freneticism of the festive season and the cold weather ahead. Prepare this boozy chocolate pudding on one of those long winter evenings and make your kitchen a safe haven from the dreariness outside. Let the windows dull with steam, wait for the heavy scent of sweetness to fill the air and sit warm by the cooker in perfect calm.

I've given instructions for steaming this pudding as I find this gives the best texture and helps to keep the pudding moist. But if you're short of time or nervous about steaming, you can bake it instead. Prepare the pudding basin and batter as below, and cover with baking parchment as instructed (even in the oven, this will help to keep some moisture in). Bake at 180°C/fan 160°C/gas mark 4 for 40–50 minutes.

First prepare the steamer: if you have a real steamer, get that set up; to improvise a stove-top steamer, fill a large pan with a couple of inches of water and place a trivet or an inverted saucer in it (this will keep the pudding basin from touching the base of the pan). Grease the pudding basin and place a circle of baking parchment in the bottom, to help with unmoulding later. Have a couple of sheets of baking parchment and a length of string to hand.

Melt the chocolate gently in a heatproof bowl in the microwave or suspended over a pan of simmering water, then set aside to cool slightly. Cream the butter and sugar together in a large mixing bowl until fluffy. Stir in the melted chocolate and the egg.

In a separate bowl, stir together the flour, baking powder, bicarbonate of soda, cocoa powder and salt. Lightly fold the dry ingredients into the chocolatey butter mixture and once they're almost combined, add the stout. Whisk gently until the batter is smooth. Pour into the prepared pudding basin. Take two sheets of baking parchment together, then fold a wide pleat into them. Perch this double-thickness of parchment on top of the pudding basin, with the pleat running across the middle (this will give the pudding room to expand as it cooks). Fold the edges of the baking parchment down over the basin and use a piece of string to wrap tightly around the rim to secure the parchment in place.

Serves 6

For the pudding:

50g dark chocolate

100g unsalted butter, softened

125g soft dark brown sugar

1 large egg

125g plain flour

1 teaspoon baking powder

¼ teaspoon bicarbonate of soda

3 tablespoons cocoa powder

Pinch of salt

125ml stout

For the sauce:

50g dark chocolate

100g soft dark brown sugar

2 tablespoons cocoa powder

50ml double cream

50ml stout

Pinch of salt

0.8–1 litre pudding basin

Turn on the steamer or place your improvised steaming pan over a medium heat. Lower the pudding basin into it and cover with a tight-fitting lid. Let the water begin to simmer, then steam for 1¼–1¾ hours, or until a knife inserted into the centre of the pudding comes out with no more than a couple of crumbs clinging to it. Remember to top up the water in the steamer regularly throughout the cooking time.

To unmould the pudding, remove the parchment covering, run a knife around the edge of the pudding, place a plate upside-down over the top of the basin and deftly flip the lot to turn the pudding out onto the plate.

As the pudding approaches the end of its cooking time, prepare the sauce. Finely chop the chocolate then set it aside. Stir the sugar and cocoa powder together, then slowly mix in the double cream, stout and salt. Heat in a small pan until scalding, then pour over the chopped chocolate and stir until smooth. Serve hot with the steamed pudding.

FIGS AND WHITE WINE MASCARPONE CREAM

Good dessert needn't be complicated. Choose ripe figs for this: if they've got a pale bloom on their skins and the pinch of your fingers dimples their flesh – all the better.

Preheat the oven to 180°C/fan 160°C/gas mark 4.

Arrange the fig halves, cut side up, in a baking tray or oven dish. Whisk the wine and sugar together and drizzle it over the figs. Roast in the oven for 10–12 minutes.

While the figs cook, whip the cream with the sugar and wine until it holds soft peaks. Beat the mascarpone until smooth in a separate bowl, then fold into the cream mixture. Serve each person three fig halves, a big dollop of the cream and a drizzle of any juices from the baking tin.

Serves 4
6 figs, halved
3 tablespoons white wine
1 tablespoon caster sugar

For the mascarpone cream:
100ml double cream
25g caster sugar
1 tablespoon white wine
100g mascarpone

More recipes with booze:
Lemon Courgette Risotto with Summer Herbs, page 145
Steamed Beef and Ale Pudding, page 246
Cider-spiked Fish Pie, page 274

INDEX

Ruby Tandoh entered *Great British Bake Off* aged just twenty. She quickly impressed with her creative approach to ingredients and flavour taking precedence over decoration. Ruby subsequently wrote a weekly food column for the *Guardian* for two years, has written columns for British *ELLE* and has made documentaries for BBC Radio 4. Her first book, *Crumb*, was published in 2014. She spends her time in Southend-on-Sea cooking, eating and watching *Take Me Out*.

She can be found at @rubytandoh

Cover design by Hyperkit
Photography by Charlotte Bland

Chatto & Windus
Vintage
20 Vauxhall Bridge Road
London SW1V 2SA
penguin.co.uk/vintage